VIEWS FROM A WESTERN-TRAINED DOCTOR IN CHINA

Past, Present and Future

Professor Patrick Chu

HKU Shenzhen Hospital

Copyright © Patrick Chu 2020
This book is sold subject to the condition that it shall not, by way of trade or otherwise, be lent, resold, hired out, or otherwise circulated without the publisher's prior consent in any form of binding or cover other than that in which it is published and without a similar condition including this condition being imposed on the subsequent publisher.
The moral right of Patrick Chu has been asserted.
ISBN-13: 9798665696522

This book has not been created to be specific to any individual's or organisation's situation or needs. Every effort has been made to make this book as accurate as possible. This book should serve only as a general guide and not as the ultimate source of subject information. This book contains information that might be dated and is intended only to educate and entertain. The author shall have no liability or responsibility to any person or entity regarding any loss or damage incurred, or alleged to have incurred, directly or indirectly, by the information contained in this book.

DEDICATION

*Dedicated to the late Sir Professor David Todd -
my life-long teacher and my moral compass.*

Dear King Ho,

*Patrick.
2020.8.1.*

CONTENTS

SPECIAL NOTE i
PREFACE 1
INTRODUCTION 4

PART 1: ON CHINA 10
    CHAPTER 1 *The Understanding and Misunderstanding of China* 10
    CHAPTER 2 *The Birth of Modern-Day China* 18
    CHAPTER 3 *Emergence from the Third World* 25
    CHAPTER 4 *Lessons Along the Way* 30
    CHAPTER 5 *Sovereignty* 37
    CHAPTER 6 *Technology Catch Up and Trend Settings in 21st-Century China.* 54

PART 2: ON MY WORK 66
    CHAPTER 7 *A Brief Description of Shenzhen* 66
    CHAPTER 8 *A Brief Description of HKU SZH* 72
    CHAPTER 9 *Preparations for the Journey* 74
    CHAPTER 10 *A General Discussion on Health Services in China* 81
    CHAPTER 11 *The First Three Years – from Nothing to Something* ... 94
    CHAPTER 12 *Commissioning of the First 24/7 Interventional Services for Ischaemic Stroke in the Department of Neurology, HKU SZH* 116
    CHAPTER 13 *My Observations* 121
    CHAPTER 14 *The Role of Traditional Chinese Medicine* 125
    CHAPTER 15 *Access to Drugs* 129
    CHAPTER 16 *Principles in the Pricing and Charging of Services in Shenzhen* . 133

CHAPTER 17 *Medical Complaints, Disputes, and Violence* *141*

CHAPTER 18 *The Use of Red Packets* *149*

CHAPTER 19 *Bonus Culture* *153*

CHAPTER 20 *Clinical Competence and Expertise* *158*

CHAPTER 21 *Over-Investigations and Over-Prescriptions* *162*

CHAPTER 22 *Choice, Flexibility, and Competition* *167*

CHAPTER 23 *Undergraduate and Postgraduate Specialty Training* *177*

CHAPTER 24 *Medical Research* *184*

PART 3: COVID-19 191

    CHAPTER 25 *From Endemic to Pandemic* *191*

PART 4: MY RECOLLECTIONS AND REFLECTIONS 219

    CHAPTER 26 *An Overseas Chinese* *219*

    CHAPTER 27 *My Rewards* *226*

    CHAPTER 28 *The Future* *232*

EPILOGUE 248

RECOMMENDED READING LIST 249

SPECIAL NOTE

COVID-19: A GLOBAL CRISIS

As I was putting in the finishing touch for this book in March 2020, there was the Wuhan Coronas Viral outbreak, the virus is now designated by WHO as COVID-19. The epicentre was in Wuhan in China and it started from December 2019. It rapidly spread from Wuhan to the rest of China within a matter of weeks. By February 2020, the total cases in China surpassed 78,000, with the bulk of cases being in Wuhan. This was a national crisis. The speed of the spread was scary. By March, countries like Korea, Japan, Italy, and Iran were also affected. By April, the highest number of confirmed cases and death were recorded in Europe and the USA. Without doubt, this was the biggest peace-time crisis the world has ever seen, at a speed which surpassed the Spanish Flu in 1918. The world was not only in shock but in a shutdown mode too, where nearly everything was closed except medical services.

I arrived back in Shenzhen at the height of the crisis in early February and witnessed first-hand the national effort in tackling this crisis. Wuhan went into lockdown. All over China, the central government, the local governments, and the citizens took collective and determined actions in facing this crisis. There was fortitude and solidarity, acts of courage and selflessness. Initially, there was despair among the people in Wuhan. The despair came from a lack of medical facilities, lack of infection-control tools such as masks, caps, and gowns, lack of hospital beds for the ill patients and logistics support for all other daily essentials. There were unprecedented efforts made by the government to support Wuhan and other cities. Huge voluntary donations were made by private enterprises and individuals in items such as food, masks, drinks, everything that one may need in times of difficulty.

Initially my families were against me coming back, but I reassured them I would be taking precautions, most importantly wearing mask, washing hands, and self-isolation all the time! This became the standard from which I am judged as a doctor, and quite rightly so. My own hospital, the Hong Kong University Shenzhen Hospital (HKU SZH), took proactive and extensive measures to deal with this crisis, especially in the prevention and early identification of any suspected cases. I think they did an outstanding job. By early March 2020, the situation came under control and I was hoping that by April, China could start the journey to recovery. The road ahead is long, but I feel very confident that Chinese people will come out good once again through their resilience, as I hope for the rest of the world too. During this sad and worrying period, lives were lost, including some front-line medical staff, who died in line of their duties. I often think about them and pray for them.

Needless to say, there are many, and there will be many more articles and books written about this COVID-19. But from my point of view, it is worth writing an extra chapter to give an account on my own experience of working in a hospital in China at the height of the crisis as a doctor and then back in the UK as a citizen living through the height of the crisis in a Western country.

PREFACE

I would like to start by saying a few words about the Medical Faculty of the University of Hong Kong (HKU) on how its history was linked with events in China and how the key stakeholders, who were the founding fathers of the Faculty, played such a key role in shaping and carving out a chapter in the history of Western medicine in China and Hong Kong. These founding fathers also influenced me greatly in my life as a medical doctor. This story started from the setting up of my beloved Medical Faculty, in a historical background landscapes of wars, famines, and widespread poverty, with much human sufferings and uncertainties in China, to the Medical Faculty at HKU, beginning its metamorphosis to become an outstanding centre of medical education with international success, recognition, and admiration in the modern world of Western medicine.

The origin of the Medical Faculty at HKU can be traced back to the Hong Kong College of Medicine for Chinese which was established in 1887 and later renamed the Hong Kong College of Medicine in 1907. This was founded by Professor Patrick Manson, a Scottish graduate from Aberdeen from the United Kingdom (UK) and who later became widely regarded as the Founder of Modern Tropical Medicine. During his time, Dr Sun Yat-sen was one of the few students in the Faculty. Dr Sun himself was a native of Guangdong and who later played a key part in the overthrow of the Qing Dynasty in 1911, and so was regarded as the founder of New China. In 1911, the then College of Medicine became officially the Medical Faculty at the University of Hong Kong. This was the start of the introduction of a structured, curriculum-based Western medical education in Hong Kong. Up to that point, most Chinese in Hong Kong, just like their compatriots in China, mainly relied on traditional Chinese medicine for treatment of diseases and ailments. At that time, China was in turmoil and Hong Kong was a British Colony. Modern Western medicine, as it was then, was denied to nearly all Chinese in Hong Kong apart from the privileged few.

My mentor Sir David Todd was born in 1928 in Guangzhou, the capital of Guangdong Province. He was placed in an orphanage during the very difficult and tumultuous times of suffering in China from civil wars, Japanese invasion, and widespread famine. Sir David was adopted as a baby by an American missionary couple, Dr Paul Todd, who was a medical doctor, and his wife Margaret Todd, who was a nurse. Dr Paul Todd was instrumental in introducing Western medicine into China, especially in Guangdong Province, where his efforts had helped the setting up of the Kung Yee Medical School in 1909. The Kung Yee Medical School later was taken over by the government and was merged with other medical schools to form the Sun Yat-sen University Medical School in Guangzhou. It is now one of the top medical schools in China. For Sir David, it was during this period of growing up with his adopted parents that he saw first-hand how Western medicine was practised, how it was taught and also the personal human sufferings he witnessed that he wanted to become a doctor, thus following the aspirations and footsteps of his adopted father, Dr Paul Todd. Sir David could have gone to the top medical school in China, known as the Peking Union Medical College, but instead he chose to study medicine at HKU in 1947. Upon graduation with honours, he joined the teaching staff at the University Department of Medicine at Queen Mary Hospital in 1953. He started his career there and worked there until his retirement.

At HKU, Sir David offered more than 40 years of selfless service and total dedication to clinical medicine, to teaching, and to research. He laid the foundation in propelling the Medical Faculty at HKU to become the much-admired institution with international fame. He was an inspiration to all of us from the Medical Faculty at HKU. He was truly a giant amongst men. His legacy is unsurpassed.

I became Sir David's student in 1973 and, years later, became his friend too. I got to know how much he relished his Guangdong roots and how much he cared about medical practices and education not only in Hong Kong but more so in China, which after all, was his homeland, though he never taught or practised medicine there. This left me with a deep impression which I have huge personal respect for. He was a legend and when Sir David passed away in 2017, he left behind, for all of us, a legacy. A legacy which, together with the other pioneers like Patrick Manson, Dr Paul Todd, and Dr Sun Yat-sen, demonstrated in no uncertain terms how the fate and well-being of Hong Kong were inextricably linked to China and vice versa. Together, China and Hong Kong can help and inspire each other, serving as a model for each other. While I do not have the privilege of knowing all these founding fathers, I do know Sir David. Such was the way he was held in the highest regards by all that I personally will feel immeasurably privileged if my life as a doctor, however insignificantly it may be, can somehow be modelled on part of his legacy, and in particular, of what it is like to be a doctor in China. I very much hope, and secretly think, that this may be a book he would have liked to read. This is why this book is dedicated to him.

INTRODUCTION

I was born in Shanghai, China in 1954. At the age of three, my parents took me, along with my two brothers and three sisters, me being the youngest, one by one, over a period of four years, to Hong Kong. I can still recall the *hutong* (a small communal space shared with others outside a house) and the barrels for water from the well in our *hutong*, fetched on a regular basis, to be boiled by wood fire back then in Shanghai. I admire and deeply appreciate my parents' determination, their effort, and their total selflessness in bringing us up.

In Hong Kong, we lived in a flat in Waterloo Road, Kowloon. Though due to the families' size, as there were also my grandmother and uncle, we often had to live apart. The families were in constant search of additional, live-able accommodation. We were not rich by any means, but we were not poverty-stricken either.

The one vivid image for an impressionable three-year-old child, on arriving in Hong Kong in December 1957, was the sight of a moving choo-choo train under a glittering and brightly lit Christmas tree which was decorated with lights of various colours. It was marvellous, so new, so exciting. This image will stick in my mind forever. This was an image of joy, homeliness, happiness, and celebration. That was my first experience of Christmas and Hong Kong.

Education then followed. Kindergarten, various primary schools, then secondary school, and finally being accepted into the Medical Faculty in the University of Hong Kong in 1973. At the time, there was only one medical school with intakes of about 150 medical students annually. The grades required for admission to the only medical school in Hong Kong (population then was four million) were so high and tough that, up to a few years ago, it was still a regular theme in my dreams in which I had failed to complete my preparation for an examination, or unable to prove a physical formula or a mathematical solution to get the top grades. This unfelt pressure, I later found out, was not uncommon at all among those who wished to go for tertiary education, especially in a competitive and scarcely resourced society like Hong Kong. I guess I was lucky then.

On finishing my internship in Hong Kong, I went to the United Kingdom in 1980, for reasons which were not too apparent for me at the time, other than wanting a change of environment. Maybe it was a sort of youthful adventurism, seen by some as misplaced intention and impatience, to try to test oneself in a slightly different world. The word 'slightly' was used deliberately here as Hong Kong was then a British Colony. The Medical Faculty at Hong Kong University was regarded as an equivalent, if not higher, standard than those in the UK. Medicine was taught, and still is, in English. Since the system of undergraduate medical education was essentially the British model, therefore those of us who wished to go to the UK did not need to take an examination to obtain another practising licence. Licence was automatically granted by the UK General Medical Council, unlike the US system, where taking and passing a licensing examination were obligatory.

I have always thought that going to the UK for me was just a short-term impulse to experience and once this experience was sampled and tasted, then I would return to Hong Kong to launch my career. I could never have imagined that I would be there for more than 32 years, thus spending a large chunk of my life there. During these years, I got promoted, got married, and had a son. In these 32 years, I went from being a trainee doctor to being a consultant haematologist, appointed honorary professor and an associate medical director in a university hospital, thus inadvertently entered into what some would call my comfort zone. I guessed I was lucky again.

'Comfort zone' are two words that I like, with some reservations. It suggests that one is possibly reaping a just and well-deserved reward for dedication and hard work long performed. But then equally it can trap one into a state of mind which is lacking in imagination, devoid of motives and desires for worthy, daring human endeavours.

It was in the autumn of 2011 when I read in the news in Hong Kong that the University of Hong Kong (HKU) would collaborate with the local government in the southern Chinese city of Shenzhen, just north of the border from Hong Kong, to run a new 2,000-bedded hospital. This was part of a national modernisation programme, as a leading project in introducing reforms in the healthcare sector. I read it with a passing interest.

Three months later, I received a call and then an approach from HKU to see if I would be interested in coming back and working in this new hospital, now named as the Hong Kong University Shenzhen Hospital (HKU SZH). I guess that I was approached not only as a haematologist, but also in the 32 years of working experience in the UK NHS (National Health Service) I managed to acquire some experience in management, service developments, undergraduate and postgraduate training, and some clinical research, especially clinical trials.

August has always been an important month of the year for me. It marks the anniversary of my wedding in 1990 and my arrival in China in 2012. The idea of writing this book was also first suggested by a respected friend and then formulated in my mind in August 2019. Sadly, it was also in the month of August 2017 when a very key figure in my life, the late Sir David Todd, passed away. Sir David taught me not only medicine and the practice of it, but above all, humanity. He was an instrumental figure in my life.

All books of this nature are subjective. This book is not an exception. It is my attempt, both descriptive and reflective, in explaining the why's, the what's, the how's of this journey and then hopefully leading to an honest effort to assess how things may turn out in the future. Each chapter can be read on its own, without interrupting the overall narrative. I hope that the collection of these chapters can lead to a better appreciation and understanding of China and the challenges China is facing and its efforts in overcoming such challenges.

First and foremost, this would require my, and perhaps the readers', need to understand the basic history and the social economic conditions in China prior to the 1980s and the huge reforms undertaken by China since then. These reforms are still very much in progress to the present day. Such an understanding is essential in enabling one to appreciate the huge progress that has already been made, plus the constant need for adjustments and improvisations along the way. Most importantly for me is how, as a practising clinician, I get to be actively involved to see things as an outsider first and then as an insider, with a ringside seat in shaping the events and happenings. It helps me to reconnect with China. This unique experience and observation form the ideas of this book. I guess I am lucky again here, for the third time, in being able to share this experience with the readers.

The narrative in this book is briefly divided into three major parts. The first part of the book is to lay the foundation for understanding modern China from a historical, political, and cultural perspective. The second part of the book is to describe the provision of health services in China and its evolution, with particular emphasis on how HKU SZH has contributed to the reforms in health services. In the 1960s, the words 'barefoot doctors' were showcased to the world. This concept of barefoot doctors was to train people with basic knowledge of hygiene and send them to the rural villages to serve the poor masses. Since then things have changed almost beyond recognition in China! Finally, in the third part, there will be some reflections of my journey and an attempt in making some predictions on what the future holds.

My writings here are not through hearsay or myth, but through the precious and genuine experience of working as a Western-trained doctor in China since 2012. I hope the combination of the three parts in this book can help the readers, both doctors and non-doctors alike, to appreciate and understand China better. It is an opportunity for me to write about the China that I came to know with deep affection. I have lived through and experienced life in a modern city in China, through my day-to-day professional and social interactions with patients, colleagues, and ordinary people. I have made friends too.

So, the story is told here, with honesty and humility, of observations made against a landscape of significant global changes politically, economically, socially, and environmentally. Most importantly, against a background of huge and unprecedented medical-technological advances mankind has ever known. I have also decided that there would not be any references at the end of this book as all the figures and facts written in this book are widely available in the public domain, while the rest are personal views and experiences to be shared. As such, there will be no graphs, no pie charts, nor any comparative data illustrations. However, I have included at the end of this book a personal recommendation of a list of books which I have read, found informative and impartial. In addition, a book of this nature will inevitably contain facts of which the readers may disagree or dispute, for which I will accept and apologise hence, as the errors in interpretation will be mine.

Finally, not being a professional or even an amateur writer, I feel both brave and handicapped. This book has consumed me with nervousness, anxiety, and trepidation, not because of its worthiness but because of my failure in telling a story, a story which needs to be told and shared. My naivety and inexperience in this are, thankfully, helped by a number of good friends and learned scholars, some of whom are still active and well-known current writers with great achievements. Their extensive knowledge in such matters not only unfailingly provides me constantly with guidance and advice, but also with admirable tolerance and patience, much like an experienced headmaster teaching a clueless student in his first day of term at school. I feel so personally encouraged by and indebted to them all. I tell them repeatedly of my heartfelt gratitude but out of my respect for their deserved privacy, as some are still well-known public figures, I shall not name them, they do know who they are and there are so many of them.

PART 1: ON CHINA

CHAPTER 1

The Understanding and Misunderstanding of China

By common consent, China is one of the earliest and longest continued civilisations in the world with a history dated back to about 5,000 years. While knowing and studying her long history are demanding, understanding her history is even harder. This civilisation is not only is characterised by its length, but by its complexity and versatility as well. It was once mentioned by a commentator that on matters related to China, the opinions one forms in the morning can be entirely different in the evening, and yet both opinions can be valid, depending on the perspective from which these opinions are formed. There are so many factors to consider!

The Influence of the Sages

One starting point perhaps is the notion that this civilisation is not bound by any dominant religious belief, unlike many other civilisations, but by a group of philosophers or sages who advocated various forms of interaction between heaven and earth. There is a form of governance with principles and rules, an orderly, hierarchical society on how the rule and the ruled should behave.

Notably among them is Confucius, a philosopher, a master teacher and political scientist, some 2,500 years ago. At that time, China was not united but rather going through a period known as the Warring States, in which there were seven separate regional powers. There was no unified order as such and this period of uncertainties and social disorders proved to be a period where various schools of philosophies first emerged in China, among which Confucianism became the most dominant one. He preached the principle that the governance of this civilisation stems from a concept of Mandate from Heaven. This mandate embraces the concept that individuals or institutions have a specific code of personal and social behaviour with specific responsibilities and a specific set of moral conduct both in the family and society. There is a hierarchical system which defines the roles and expected behaviour of individual members in families on issues related to parenthood, filial attitude towards the parents, respect and the rituals of respect to the ancestors, friendship, justice, fairness, and morality, all are necessary in creating a harmonious and stable society. In other words, there is the prerequisite need of a form of anticipated obedience which is in equilibrium and exists side by side with expected benevolent autocracy of the rulers as a core principle of a dynasty. It is the Mandate from Heaven and the practice of benevolent autocracy that give the ruling class its legitimacy. A harmonious society requires contribution from both sides, the right code for the rulers and the ruled. It is a form of social contract. This is a concept very different from Western civilisation that originated from Ancient Greece. Power is not necessarily shared but bestowed and therefore an abuse of power must be avoided. Dynastic rules can come and go but this benevolent autocracy is the requirement from which the mandate was granted and legitimised. This Confucianism became the dominant philosophy throughout Chinese history. The essential teachings of Confucius were later compiled by his students to form a classic called *The Analects*. There are now also Schools of Confucianism abroad to promote further understanding of this philosophy.

In addition, there is also the very ritualistic philosophy of Taoism, founded roughly around the same time. Taoists believe that people can become deities or live forever through practising certain rituals and the difference between nature and humans is minimal or even non-existent, thus achieving nothingness or fullness through celestial harmony and cosmic equilibrium. The other major influence in the Chinese civilisation is a book called the *I Ching*, or commonly known as the *Book of Changes*. *I Ching* deals not so much on philosophy but tries to explain and explore the meaning of life rather on metaphysical and cosmological terms. It is regarded as one of the oldest books ever written, estimated to be dated in the late Shang or early Zhou Period about 3,000 years ago, even before Confucianism and Taoism. *I Ching* emphasises divinity and earthly events and how their interrelationship can somehow be explained by predictable cyclical and mythical means through the use of symbols or diagrams, mainly hexagonal in nature. *I Ching* can also be regarded as a form of mathematical text which can be used in prediction for future events. Some would even regard this as a possible origin of the binary system in the modern digital world: The *Yin* and the *Yang*, the lightness and darkness, the fire and the wood, the positive and the negative. The teachings of Confucius were thought to be influenced by *I Ching*. There are other schools too, such as Mencius and Zhuangzi. All emphasise a way of interaction between divinity, personal conduct, social behaviour, morals, and dynastic governance in search of harmony under heaven. The Mandate from Heaven is closely linked directly with Peace and Harmony on Earth.

Some aspects of these thoughts can be unexplainable, especially in the absence of an all-creating God, unlike many other religions. Heaven is the concept instead. So, for instance, natural disasters such as major earthquakes, famines, and floods were often interpreted as having a hidden meaning as messages from heaven, signalling that the equilibrium between the all-important dynastical benevolence and anticipatory obedience was no longer there. Therefore, this could be viewed as a punishment from Heaven and so went the mandate to rule. This profound cultural belief based on Confucianism, odd it may be seen in the present world, was officially endorsed by the Han Dynasty as the state philosophy about 2,300 years ago. There has never been a state religion in China, but this state philosophy known as Confucianism came as close to the equivalence of religion dominance seen in other civilisations. This Confucius philosophy was indeed the very fundamental and dominant moral compass throughout the years of Chinese civilisation.

While Taoism, also very popular, emphasises rituals and a state of mind and thoughts of divinity of an individual in another world, Confucianism stresses actions and behaviours of an individual. Even at the times of the non ethnic Chinese dynasties, such as the Yuan (tribes from Mongolia) and Qing (tribes from Northeast China known as the Manchu) Dynasties, such a Confucius-based school of governance was still by and large adhered to and practised. Thus, Confucianism can be regarded as a sort of 'Practical Rule Book' for the roles and interaction between the governed, the governing, and heaven.

A Vast Landmass with Limited Resources

Yet one important practical difficulty in a civilisation which practised such benevolent autocracy by the rulers and thus anticipatory obedience from the ruled has to cope with is China's large and ever-increasing population. This difficulty is about the importance of agriculture and provision of food for the people. The ever-expanding population, evolving from villages to walled towns to the formation of major cities in a civilisation which for thousands of years was primarily agricultural in nature, poses an ever-present challenge. This is a perpetual but very difficult problem to be solved. Confucianism preaches mainly behaviour and attitude, emphasising the right balance will lead to harmony in society. And yet in China, we have a saying, "Of all the 100 ailments, the first one to treat is the feeling of hunger". This is so true, so apt and so basic.

I have often thought that historians, in addressing and analysing the system of governance in the history of China, its successes and failures, often overplayed its interpretation of historic events in terms of dynastic powers, its adventures, its conflicts, its military successes and failures, its creation in arts and science. Yet they often failed to explain or appreciate the essential need of feeding the people as the number one priority throughout its history. Due to China's severe shortage of arable land, farming in the country has always been very labour-intensive. In the history of China, most of the practical inventions of value were mainly agricultural in nature such as the invented tools for water drainage, water supply and irrigation. Famines could be natural or man-made, but nonetheless the prevention of famines would always be the priority for any dynastic rule. These studies of China and its history often, in my view, fail to appreciate the importance of the roles of the peasants, however uneducated they may be, in sustaining an ever-increasing population. In China, there is a traditional saying that there are four choices to make a living and, in descending order, are: literacy (for the educated), peasantry (for the farmers), craftsmanship (for the artisans), and commerce (for the businessmen). So China, with its vast population, has for thousands of years been mainly an agricultural society with farming being the second choice to make a living. The priority for the mind is in seeking knowledge while the priority for the physical body is farming for food. In fact, the main reason for the many changes in dynasty through wars and revolts throughout the history of China were primarily by the peasants, not because of harsh policies but because of famines and lack of food.

Regrettably, even the Confucius philosophy did not specifically mention this but rather assuming benevolence will include, as a matter of fact and not as a matter of importance, agricultural expansion and successes. In other words, China's agricultural challenges in feeding the people, its quests for food, its need for avoiding hunger, was not quite appreciated by most historians. When famines struck, the human sufferings were measured not in thousands but millions. This need for food and the desire not to waste any food led to some undiscerning commentators often making the headline-grabbing and soundbite message, with a hint of humiliation and ridicule, that the Chinese will eat anything that moves! To that charge, I would counter that the Chinese not only will eat anything, including things that don't move, as long as it is not poisonous! Furthermore, the Chinese would also do anything to create arable land for crops too, to increase food supply by any means and from any sources.

China, unlike the United States of America (USA), does not have, on a per capita basis, much arable land. China's landscapes and mountains are so geographically and agriculturally hostile (the only big arable land mass being the plains in the North) that expanding arable land for agriculture was impossibly hard. Innovative efforts must be made and hence the unique and ironically now picturesque popular tourist attraction sites of ladder rice fields. These may be great scenes to look at, especially the aerial shots taken from helicopters. These shots have become the main theme of many travel documentaries, photos in travelling magazines for marketing purposes and numerous postcards. But, thinking back, these fields certainly were not created for their aerial photo-opportunity to attract tourists. Far from it, these were created purely out of the absolute necessity to use every piece of arable land, however hard it may be. One does need to appreciate the reasoning behind, and the challenges and hardship involved, of creating such a tiny piece of land for agricultural needs to feed the people, not to mention the hazards of farming these tiny pieces of land in a steep mountain on a day-to-day basis. The discerning tourists may now well begin to appreciate, perhaps even ponder, the reason for the creation of the ladder rice fields. China's One Child Policy was born out of this need. Recurrent mass starvation, from famines or wars or both, in the long history of China, if not prevented, can be as deadly, with more tragic human consequences, such as abandoned new-born babies, as the deadly plague which swept across Eurasia, wiping out millions of people in the 14th century.

So, in essence, China is a civilisation which is fundamentally agricultural in nature and which believes in the legitimacy granted by the Mandate from Heaven concept in providing a framework of behaviour for the people and the rulers. This absence of dominance by any religion is in sharp contrast to other long civilisations which are influenced by Hinduism, Buddhism, Judaism, Islam, and

Christianity. Even though some religions were thought to be introduced into China as far back as the Tang Dynasty, they never took hold as the dominant belief by any dynastic rulers.

CHAPTER 2

The Birth of Modern-Day China

It is generally hard to define exactly what modern-day China means and when did it start. It is commonly accepted by most historians that modern China started when the last dynasty was overthrown, leading to the setting up of a new republic and by this definition, modern China may be seen as starting from 1912 after the collapse and end of the last imperial dynasty called the Qing Dynasty. However, the end of a dynasty after thousands of years of dynastic rule may not necessarily mean the birth of modern China in the Western sense of the word. The change in the principle of administration by a different political system of governance does not necessarily and certainly does not guarantee a change from the old to the new.

Modernity can mean different things to different people. This is especially true for China as even though the dynastic rule ended in 1912, a new national order was not successfully established afterwards. There were years of social turmoil and fighting, littered with failures after failures. Indeed, what followed were decades of political struggles and civil wars for territorial control and power. Not only were there national armed conflicts, there were also regional conflicts too, each faction imposing its own rules to govern, hence the term 'warlords'. It is often a cliché to say history always repeats itself, and we, as humans, never learn. None more so is classically illustrated by the fact that the existence of these warlords was almost an exact replica of the Warring States in China around 2,500 years ago, until the first unification of the all the states by the First Emperor Qin Shi Huang, whose common name was Yin Zheng, who established the Qin Dynasty, regarded by historians as the first ever united China in 221 BCE.

Even though the imperial history of China ended with the Qing Dynasty in 1912, the decline of the dynasty rule can be traced back to more than 70 years before that. China was then ruled by the Manchurians (a tribe who originated from Northeast China) who founded the Qing Dynasty in 1644. The Manchu rule was very much modelled, unimaginatively and passively, along the same tried-and-tested formula in which the emperor's rule was administered and implemented by mandarins. The mandarins formed a civil service structure, and to become a mandarin in the civil service, the mandatory qualification was to distinguish themselves in state-run examinations for classics and humanities. Those who scored highest would be appointed. Women were, of course, barred from such examinations. In fact, for women to be able to write, read, and be educated was regarded as not important or indeed socially undesirable in traditional Chinese civilisation. Knowledge in classics was mandatory and considered to be a gateway to senior government positions. This knowledge was also consistently and erroneously, in my view, seen as equated with ability.

This Qing Dynasty was founded in 1644, almost 100 years before the USA, which was founded in 1776. The Qing Dynasty did have its glorious days initially and made significant cultural contributions (the first ever *Imperial Dictionary for China*) and territorial expansion in the west in its early days, regarded by many historians as reaching another golden period of dynastic China. Indeed, for roughly seven centuries, from 1100, shortly after the Norman conquest of England, to around 1760, when the First Industrial Revolution took place in England,

China accounted for approximately a quarter of the global economy and was then the biggest economic power of the world. Up to that period, some historians even pointed out that as a result of its big landmass and its huge population, China was the world's biggest economy in the first 1800 years since the start of the Common Era. But then, China started its national decline and its portion of world trade had dwindled to less than 10% by the early 20th century. On the other hand, the British Empire, home of the First Industrial Revolution, invented the steam engine and the textile machine, among many other things. This dramatically increased the British Empire's industrial productivity and output. The days of machinery for production and transport had arrived. All it needed to do to expand further was to trade on its success and look for raw materials and human labour. Its machinery prowess also enabled it to develop its already advanced naval fleet as a military backup in its pursuit of trade and global economic interests. The British Empire, having thus acquired a new-found confidence, sent its emissary Lord Macartney on a diplomatic mission from the UK to China in 1793 with the objective to establish bilateral trade. He brought with him many products and presents as tributes to the then Emperor Qianlong of the Qing Dynasty. The Emperor, long indoctrinated by the notion that China was at the peak of its power, while ignorant of the advances made in other parts of the world, dismissed the effort of the emissary with the famous line, "We possess all things. I see no value in objects strange and ingenious and have no use for your country's manufactures." This conceited and self-deluded grandiose attitude later proved to be the roots of its downfall. Due to imperial overstretch, combined with complacency, and self-gratification, the Qing Dynasty gradually descended into stagnation, incompetence, and an inability to change and adapt. It portrayed for itself a self-important China-centric view based on its own assessment of its glorious past, while at the same time was grossly ignorant of worldly developments beyond the borders of China. This could not have happened at the worst possible time as it was just about the time when Western Europe, especially the UK, reached the zenith of its powers through the First Industrial Revolution. In other words, China was caught sleeping in its own glorious past. There then followed this period in Chinese history called the Century of Humiliation, which will be discussed further in Chapter 5 under the heading of Sovereignty.

The Beginning of New China

My own view, however, is that the birth of Modern China can be interpreted and traced back through two historic events. The first was in 1949 when Chairman Mao Zedong of the Chinese Communist Party (CCP) declared the birth of the People's Republic of China (PRC) after defeating the Nationalist Party which then fled to Taiwan to establish another administration. Then, China was very poor but very determined to form a united country, freed from humiliations and invasions. The second was 1979 when China declared major national commitments to reforms and opening-up (*gaige kaifang*) with the Four Modernisations Program under the then paramount leader Deng Xiaoping. Both events, though separated by 30 years, were actually interrelated. This new national path and drive towards modernisation was first discussed in the 1950s. These were set in motion throughout the early years but were interrupted by various ideological-based political movements such as the Let A Hundred Flowers Bloom, the Commune system, the Great Leap Forward, and the Cultural Revolution. All these movements, while aiming for ideological purity, often resulted in turbulence and upheavals, leading to great human suffering, starvation, stagnation of the economy, and loss of human lives. The internal debate then was not that modernisation was not needed, that much was agreed by all, but the means or models by which the program should be implemented. Should it still be the Soviet model based on a centrally planned and directed economy or should it be a US and Western European model based on a market-directed economy?

With that background, my personal preference for the start of this Modern China would be 1979. Much of the credit for this modernity, in my view, and deservedly so, goes to Deng Xiaoping, when he steered China towards reforms and opening-up. He launched this unprecedented new model of market-based reforms with an extraordinary display of uncompromising sheer willpower and determination. Mr Deng, then in his seventies, launched three major and ground-breaking initiatives in a Communist country with the world's biggest population in the late 1970s. The importance of these initiatives cannot be underestimated nor overstated. These initiatives were borne out of economic consideration for the needs of a massive but poor and backward nation. Unlike the previous initiatives, such as the Great Leap Forward or Cultural Revolution which placed ideological conviction before pragmatic economic consideration, Deng's initiatives were based on pragmatic considerations for improving the livelihood of the ordinary Chinese people, and not an ideological one, with his immortal line of: "It matters not if the cat is black or white, as long as it catches the mice, then it will be a good cat". The end will justify the means. This change of direction is gigantic and monumental, like pressing a reset button on a supercomputer, the only difference being that the computer will of course reset once the button is pressed while this tumultuous change of direction for a country as big as China takes momentum, conviction, and unwavering determination over a long and almost undefinable period of time to accomplish.

The Becoming of Modern China

Firstly, Deng reaffirmed the official commitments of the Four Modernisations Program (industry, agriculture, defence, and technology). Secondly, he launched a ground-breaking national policy of reform and opening up from a Soviet-based, state-directed, centrally planned model of economy to a Western-based, primarily the USA, market economy, in the most populous communist country in the world. He termed it 'Socialism with Chinese Characteristics'. He was the initiator and pusher for such an economic model in China. He never wavered. This major shift in policy managed to unleash the motivation, the drive, and the innovation of the individuals in communities, villages, and cities all over China. It emphasised and recognised the important economic roles of small, private enterprises rather than the previous state model of a commune where individual incentives and initiatives were replaced by collective inertia. All that was required in the commune era was to follow central planning and directives. Individualism was ignored and stifled while collectivism was emphasised. With Deng's initiatives, the reverse was now revered. The new buzzwords will be market-led enhanced productivity, resource allocations and distribution while pricing, profits, and investments are to be determined mainly by the individuals, small enterprises, and the forces of the market. A spirit of competition for performance was encouraged. Getting prosperous is not to be condemned, getting rich may even be glorious. Prosperity for all may not happen all at once, some will get richer quicker than others, but it will set a precedent and a path for others to follow. These initiatives of reforms, by common consent, were extraordinarily successful in reducing mass poverty and sustaining economic growth, and unprecedented too, on a scale never seen before in the history of mankind. Thirdly, he came up with the innovative and hitherto unheard-of and untested 'One Country, Two Systems' in the post-1997 arrangement for Hong Kong after the handover of this last remaining British colony in the Far East back to China.

Another key fact worth mentioning, especially as discussed in the previous chapter about the importance of agriculture and food supply throughout the history of China, is that about 35% of China's current labour force is in agriculture (compared to 2.5% in the USA). There are 425 million agricultural workers (200 million farming households) in China. A little over a decade ago China was home to 700 million farmers. They made up about 60 percent of the population. So, as modernisation continues apace in China, so will its advances in modern agricultural technology. I have no doubt that the productivity and output will continue to grow while the need for manual labour input will fall. This particular area of striving for agricultural self-sufficiency is not commonly discussed in the West but nonetheless is a key plank of the national policies in China.

CHAPTER 3

Emergence from the Third World

The words First, Second, and Third Worlds are now deemed by some to be irrelevant in the 21st century and the word globalisation seems to have taken its place. It was February 1974, in a meeting with a leader in a Third World country, Chairman Mao Zedong in China was reported as saying that in his view, the USA and the Soviet Union formed the First World, Japan, Europe, and Canada formed the Second World while China, along with Asia, Africa, and Latin American (the non-aligned blocks) belonged to the Third World. To a layman like me, I interpret this as a rough and broad conceptual classification based primarily on the economic, military, and political strengths. Right after WW2, the term Iron Curtain was coined to describe the Eastern European block known as the Union of Soviet Socialist Republic (USSR). As a result, the First World and the Second World were then engaged in the Cold War, which ended in 1991 with the fall of the Berlin Wall. China was poor during that period.

So, in order to fully appreciate the importance of the emergence of China from the Third World, some basic information is needed. China is now the world's second largest economy in terms of gross domestic product (GDP). From 1980 to 2015, the average GDP growth per annum for China was around 10% and from 2015 onward, the average growth was 6%. This growth has been uninterrupted, without pause, over the last 40 years and the latest estimate for the next few years is still a net growth to between 5% and

6%. These growth figures are what most modern economies and countries would die for. Nonetheless, it is important also to bear in mind that due to China's large population, the income per capita still ranks relatively low globally compared to other more advanced economies. According to the latest World Bank estimates, the average income in China still only falls into the category of top half of middle-income countries. Therefore, the need for further progress to increase the prosperity of the people necessitates the imperative of changing from a manufacturing-based economic model to a technology-based, knowledge-based, service-based economic model. In other words, China needs to climb up the value chain, just like most other advanced economies have been doing in the last two decades.

Of all the data, all the information, and all the books written about modern China and its achievements, one achievement which stands out, which fills me with the greatest emotional pride, and which impresses me most is the one which showed that, according to the definition of poverty by the United Nations, 600 million people in China had been lifted out of poverty since the Reform and Opening-up policy started in the early 1980s in China. This is a staggering and colossal achievement, never seen before in human history, never before has such a feat been achieved by any country, in any regions, by any political system at any time in the world. This statistic alone has the most profound effect on me.

This unique 'Chinese Way' of lifting people out of poverty was achieved through a variety of reasons, the discussion of which falls outside the scope of this book but it is generally agreed and accepted that this was primarily due to several reasons. First, a huge export-driven, consumer products manufacturing industry, earning the nickname 'Factory of the World' through a combination of cheap, youthful, and skilful labour force. This emerging labour force is willing to migrate to bigger metropolises and modern factories, backed up, managed, and financed by private investment in both capital and modern business management know-how. Apple did not base its iPhone manufacturing in China from just any simplistic decision on cheap labour but rather it based its decision on the supply of skilled labour, the size of the China domestic market and China's renowned expertise in supply chain logistics and exports. Second, enabling part ownership of the land by farmers with any surplus agricultural products to be sold on the open market. In short, it is a combination of making food to feed and making stuff to sell, both to a domestic and an international market, by a young, hard-working, and motivated population. Thirdly, China arrived with perfect timing in integrating itself right from the beginning of the globalisation process, almost like beginning with a clean sheet of paper, with the result that both the global community and China became the beneficiaries, leading directly to China joining the World Trade Organisation (WTO) in 2001.

The 'Made in China' Economic Model

This model was best demonstrated by the economic success in the southern city of Shenzhen, where I work. Shenzhen, with its proximity to Hong Kong, was able to tap into the expertise that Hong Kong has to offer. Over the last few decades, Hong Kong has metamorphosised itself into a major international financial centre with all its acquired and sophisticated knowledge and experience in financing, banking, accounting, and modern management. These are exactly the essential ingredients for economic reforms and progress which China needs. This geographical advantage, coupled with the determination of the Shenzhen government for economic reforms, such as the provision of cheap labour and tax incentives, was a major reason for its outstanding success. Right from the start, in the late 1970s, the city of Shenzhen was designated by the central government as a Special Economic Zone (SEZ) for reforms and opening-up. By 2018, within a period of 40 years, the GDP of Shenzhen has surpassed that of Hong Kong. This model of successive economic reforms and transformation was internationally widely discussed among academics, economists, and political scientists. In addition, in the last 10 years, Shenzhen has also made huge progress in climbing up the value chain from producing low-end manufactured goods, to a high-end service economy based on the practical applications of technological advances. This will be further elaborated in Chapter 6 of this book.

This Chinese economic model is not only studied widely by economists, academics, and political scientists, but also adopted by various newly emerging economies especially in Asia, Eastern Europe, and Africa. This is now viewed by some as the Beijing Consensus as an alternative developmental model, alongside the prevailing and dominant Post World War II model known as the Washington Consensus. The principle of the Washington Consensus is that the USA should organise and lead all the key pillars and systems of international institutions, governance, and financial systems. This Washington Consensus, meaning the US doctrine of liberal capitalism and prosperity through democracy, is also known as the post WWII New Liberal Order with the establishment of organisations such as the World Bank, the International Monetary Fund, and the United Nations. The first two are based in Washington and the third one is based in New York. Contrary to what some harsh critics have commented, this newly emerging perception of the Beijing Consensus is not a Chinese creation, it was created by commentators in the West. The more appropriate term in my view is the Beijing Model. It is not aimed at, or intended, by any means, to replace the Washington Consensus, which is still the dominant model. The Beijing Model may serve as an alternative model, another choice for nation states to decide, based on their own specific cultural, social, economic, and ideological needs. This is never about which is better, or which is right, it is more about which suits a nation better at a given time of its development and economic progress.

So, in just over only a few decades, in a country with 1.4 billion population, where agricultural needs were of prime importance and agricultural production was regarded historically very much as the cornerstone of economic development, China has moved from being part of the Third World to become the second largest economy in the world in terms of GDP, just behind the USA. This was done with remarkably successful and successive programmes of industrialisation, urbanisation, opening-up and modernisation, all proceeding with breakneck speed without any pause for breath. In doing so, the country has been transformed from an agricultural-based economy to an industrial-based economy, with all the pros and cons of rapid industrialisation to deal with while the Made in China label is everywhere to be seen in our day-to-day life. In my view, these unprecedented achievements are noticeable not only in their objectives, but the courage and determination to constantly revise and adjust policies in their actual implementation. A system which in the last 40 years was constantly undergoing self-adjustments and corrections has much to be admired. No model can be planned to perfection right from the start, but it is the courage to adapt, change, and persevere along the way which can see a successful model through. This model was immortalised and best described by another line from Deng: "Crossing the river by feeling the stones"!

CHAPTER 4

Lessons Along the Way

None of the remarkable economic progress can be achieved without any price. Every worthwhile human endeavour is achieved, never the easy way, but the hard way, be it scientific discoveries, artistic attainments, or technological advances. Often we see, enjoy, and benefit from the successes, and even become the direct beneficiaries of scientific achievements or appreciators of various forms of art ranging from popular music to classical literature. However, to think certain things happen by chance, by being superbly clever, or by accident is to understate the importance of hard work underpinning it, not forgetting the often despair and disappointments faced by the scientists or the artists when a hypothesis was proven wrong, an experiment gone haywire, or a painting failed to sell. History is full of these perceived failures of unsung scientists and artists, who never get noticed but all play a part in enriching our lives. Likewise, in the case of running a country, be it hereditary dynasties, one-party states, or democracies, no single social development or economic theory can prove to be predictive of an all-embracing success without price. The law of unintended consequences always applies. Political scientists term this 'the moral consequences of economic growth'. There is also a parallel in my own field of medicine. However effective a drug may be, there will always be predictable and known side effects, as well as unpredictable effects otherwise known as idiosyncratic reactions.

    The same applies to China. In her quest for economic progress, and improvement of the living standards of the people, there was bound to be growing pain. This is both predictable and unavoidable. It happens in any society and no country in the world can be exempted from the side effects of achieving prosperity of the masses. This happened in China too. By this I am specifically referring to the matching of economic prosperity in society as a whole and the achievement of wealth as an individual on the one side with that of progress in civic behaviours on the other side. In other words, would our behaviour change when we move from being poor to a state of relative prosperity? What is the downside in the pursuit of wealth? In my opinion, this downside (the growing pain) could range from failure for a driver in a posh car to stop at zebra crossing, jumping the queue for the cashier in the retail shop, sloppy workmanship and widespread copycat production of faked watches, handbags, DVDs, CDs, or even books! This fast buck culture can even spread to the production of fake drugs or poisoned baby milk. Then, there was no concept or the need for the recognition of intellectual property protection. It was very much a 'He who dares wins, fortune favours the brave' mindset. I was guilty too. I remember clearly that it was about 15 years ago when I first went to Shenzhen as a tourist in search of cheap, fake DVDs for my favourite TV shows. I now feel remorseful as I was actually inadvertently supporting and condoning this practice of faking things that may sell.

However, this situation is now much improved. It is so obvious that during my eight years of working in Shenzhen, this Law of the Jungle phenomenon described above is now changing and changing fast. Not only in Shenzhen, but in the other cities I visited too, significant improvements in civilities are very much noticeable. Queueing in shops, stopping at zebra crossings are now standard, fake watches are not openly flaunted (even hard to find!), public places are clean and not littered. Noticeably too, that whenever I walk into a busy restaurant, people always queue up outside and seats are provided for waiting customers. Consumer protection has also caught up and is now regarded as a standard practice in China. After-sale service has improved and become more efficient. In other words, trading standards and consumer protection have much improved. Recently I bought a Bluetooth earphone by mail order in China. It was delivered the next day and after four weeks, one earpiece failed to work. I was given a new replacement within a week, as my order could be so accurately checked and traced! So improvement in civic behaviour and business practices, along with economic advancement, has now caught up with each other. The progress is obvious for all to see.

Another lesson is business transparency. It was commonly assumed in China that even bilateral business transactions may have multiple hidden layers, involving third or fourth parties, with non-transparent transaction costs involving various participants. In China, this is known by some as transfer of interests, material or financial, from one participant to the other. Business practices become solely money and profits driven for all involved, while honesty and transparency may be of secondary consideration in the process. It is the efficiency, speed, and the completion of the transaction that counts. There is also, as a result of uninterrupted economic growth, the emergence of the nouveau riche who often can use personal or political connections for fast tracking business transactions, or for undeclared material or financial gain. Such widespread transfer of interests (known also as corruption) was so prevalent and deep-rooted that it was even regarded, until a few years ago, as the norm and a way of life, and oil that was needed to grease the machine. Many see this as an unavoidable side effect of modernisation and materialism, viewed not only as an acceptable but also a necessary part of standard business practice. This problem became so prevalent and widespread that it was barely accepted and tolerated by the people. It became the major social and political issue widely discussed both formally and informally within China. The situation was so dire that the President of China, Mr Xi Jinping, at being appointed as the President of the People's Republic of China in 2012, publicly launched a nationwide anti-corruption campaign on a scale never seen before, daring the wrath of the politically well-connected and the wealthy. People of various backgrounds, businessmen, politicians, senior and junior government officials were sent to trials in court and imprisoned if found guilty with their ill-gotten wealth confiscated. This campaign was very successful and widely applauded by the people. It is highly commendable to note that this nationally targeted anti-corruption drive, daring in its approach and determined in its execution, is now having a significant and positive impact in the whole country. Laudable articles and commentaries are regularly written and published in national or local press and in social media. Even television dramas on the national anti-corruption campaign received widespread applause and thumbs up with high viewing figures. To me, this is a significant achievement.

Impact on the Environment

The relentless pace and the scale of the industrialisation and economic progress also exert a significant effect on climate change and the environment. China, together with the USA, contribute to 40% of the world's global carbon dioxide emissions. The massive industrialisation and infrastructure building programmes have led to concerns about the destruction of natural wildlife habitat with huge ecological damage to the environment. Survival for some species is threatened. Air pollution is worse and gets more and more problematic in all the major cities such as Beijing, Shanghai, and Guangzhou. Our whole ecosystem is under threat. Massive state public education efforts on the importance of environmental protection are being made and the efforts are now bearing fruit. People are more and more aware of the need for protecting the environment collectively, actively, and consciously. These days, when I go on a walkabout in Shenzhen, I can easily notice that more and more shoppers in supermarkets are now using recycled bags and not plastic bags. Their shoulder bags are made from eco-friendly materials and not plastics. Every shop around the corner is beginning to reduce plastic consumption, and every citizen is encouraged to use eco-friendly products.

In this key area of protecting the environment, China is one of the most vocal and proactive advocates in adopting an eco-friendly developmental model. In 2016, China attended the Paris Accord on Climate Change. This Accord led to an international agreement with 195 signatures of states on dealing with climate change and agreed on a long-term global target of keeping the increase in global average temperature to 1.5 degree centigrade. Under this agreement, each country must determine, plan, and regularly report on the contribution it undertakes to mitigate global warming. In China, it is obvious that the commitments made in the Paris Accord are being honoured and actively implemented by both the government departments and private enterprises. Eight years ago, when I first arrived in Shenzhen, 90% of the taxis were red cabs, the traditional petrol-driven cars, and now more than 95% of the taxis are the more comfortable, quieter home-made electric cars. Take for instance another example, China is now leading the world in high-speed electric power trains which is one of the more successful export industries. I take these high-speed trains regularly, and they are amazingly comfortable, spacious, and clean. The protection of the environment and the tackling of climate change are now a high priority government policy. In my own work at HKU SZH, I have been involved in the planning of some major capital projects for the hospital in the last few years and for every one of these projects I witnessed how its environmental impact was thoroughly assessed and studied stringently.

Furthermore, despite its size and traditional mode of energy production based on the burning of coal, China has made huge strides in the use of clean, alternative energy and is now the world's leading country in electricity production from renewable energy sources, ahead of the USA, mainly from hydroelectric and wind power. Its capacity is growing faster than fossil fuels or even nuclear energy. In 2018, China's renewable energy consumption was 38% higher than that of the USA and triple that of Germany. Presently, the use of renewables is growing by 25% per year in the last five years, and if this trend is maintained, then the renewables will reach 20% of China's total energy consumption by 2025! However, there is still a long way to go and much work still needs to be done as the energy requirement is so huge because of the high demands from the large population and national infrastructure needs. Eco-friendly projects are encouraged and supported by the state and the local governments with tax incentives. 'Go Green' is a popular motto used and promoted by institutions such as hospitals, especially the HKU SZH. In a city like Shenzhen, more than 95% of the taxis are the blue electric cars, with low carbon footprint, implemented successfully by proactive local government policies which invested heavily and wisely in providing very easy access to public charging points for the drivers. Talking to the drivers, nearly all of them tell me that after switching over to electric cars, they don't want to switch back to traditional petrol cars. Furthermore, technological innovation means that it is almost inevitable that battery technology will be better and last longer, while charging will be quicker, and electric cars will be the norm and not the exception. Indeed, this modern relevance of the chargeable battery technology is fully recognised by awarding the Nobel Prize in Chemistry in 2019 to three scientists for their pioneering work on lithium ion batteries in the 1970s, which laid the foundation for the development of mobile, storable, and renewable energy, free from the environmental-damaging fossil energy.

CHAPTER 5

Sovereignty

This is an enormously important subject worthy of discussion separately. Indeed, this issue of China and its sovereignty since the 1840s has been the title of a book published as recently as July 2019 by the Cambridge University Press. It is a very timely and important piece of scholarly work. It emphasises how China broadens its own views on modern history by looking at and studying intensely the meaning of sovereignty by its political leaders, intellectuals, and diplomats. In doing so, they challenged the concept and the interpretation of sovereignty in international law, which was historically an interpretation based on Western Eurocentric views, and which fails to consider the positions and the cultures of the non-Europeans. So just like a coin, there are always two sides!

This revision of a conventionally accepted view is timely and worth noting. There is also in recent years the emergence of another view, especially among the academic historians, that most accounts of world history are also primarily based on a Eurocentric view. For example, the terms 'Far East' and 'Middle East' originated from a Eurocentric perspective with Europe being the reference point. There is a need for a reappraisal and a view of history from a different angle. Books, whose views are essentially from a non-Eurocentric view, have now been published to wide international acclaim for their academic rigour and their alternative interpretations. Some authors of these books took a view of history, especially of the

Old World, based on the Silk Road culture of trades stretching and covering huge and inhospitable land masses, from China and India in Asia to Central Asia, the Middle East, and all the way to Europe. The Silk Road is famous not only for its trade, as trading is as old as civilisation itself, but it was the first human endeavour to engage in trades across continents and cultures. It is a modern-day equivalent of globalisation in the absence of sea or air routes, motor vehicles, electricity, or common languages. Furthermore, the trades were mainly conducted between the people of different faiths stretching westwards from the non-religious Chinese, to the religious Indians, to the Muslims, Jews, and even as far as the Christians in Europe. I see this as a Silk Road Culture. A culture which was distinguished by a giant kaleidoscope of buyers and sellers on a remarkable range of goods over a remarkably long period of time and over a huge landmass, and yet this culture was not marred by any major recorded events of violence and clashes among people from different backgrounds. The American continents were not even discovered then. The other aspect is that even though it was started initially by the Han Dynasty around 130 BCE, it continued to flourish and reached its zenith by the Yuan Dynasty (the Mongols who ruled China then, famous for their horse-riding skills and thus mobility) until it was boycotted by the Ottoman Empire in 1453. The Yuan Empire moved westwards to the vast area in Central Asia, and almost to the present-day Western Europe. Yet with this territorial expansion by the Mongols, there were no major recorded events which led to large scale clashes of civilisations. Each participant or culture involved would have engaged in wars, blood sheds, and periods of subordination but the Mongols were not there for long and the sovereignty of the conquered states, as it were, were not significantly threatened. In other words, looking at these events from the conventional perspective, the concept and the ideas of sovereignty were not widely recognised in the past. The prevailing concept at the time was the idea of Empires and Emperors, from the Roman Empire in the West, to the Ottoman Empire in Central Asia, and the Yuan Empire in Mongolia. In short, sovereignty is a relatively recent concept in the context of history.

What is Sovereignty?

To a layman like me, sovereignty is the full right of a governing body over itself, without any interference, political or military, from outside sources or bodies. It embodies the connotations of independence, self-determination, territorial integrity, mutual respect for other nation states, and the avoidance of interference on the policies, especially domestic policies of other nations. These are the five key benchmarks. Interference at best can be seen as condescension by lecturing or preaching between nations or at worst, conspiratorial and interpreted as barely hidden ill intentions from those who do the lecturing to those being lectured to. There may even be a degree of duplicity there, which can be interpreted as: "Do what I say but don't do what I do". So, pursuit of national strategic, political, economic dominance and interests can often be disguised through the distorted lens of a certain degree of moral superiority. The concept of sovereignty for a nation broadly means that any nation would rightfully expect and require a definite degree of respect, non-interference, and tolerance from other nations within the framework of international law and diplomacy. For example, I may not like the way the neighbours down the road dress or the food they eat or the way they decorate their house, but I would never venture a negative opinion on them out of my respect for them to live the way they want, as long as it is within the law of the country they live in. Sovereignty, to put it bluntly, is similar. In this world, we all try to be good neighbours and should behave as such.

On the other hand, this can equally be used as a defence against criticism, especially when the criticisms touch on sensitive areas such as the five benchmarks mentioned above. These defences are often made by diplomats or political leaders to justify and explain policies and actions to the outside world, but also to mobilise support from the masses on the side being criticised. Depending on how this is handled, the consequences can vary from patriotism for the love of a country to fervent and misguided nationalism, thus changing an outward looking country to an inward looking one. As mentioned in previous chapters, the late Qing Dynasty was also marked by this inward-looking shift in its outlook, leading to its eventual demise.

Since the birth of modern China, at different times of its very short and often turbulent history (the People's Republic of China was established in 1949), there were various comments, political rhetoric and statements made by others on China, especially from the West. Most of these comments on China and its policies were made based on the ideological differences between China and the West. The one case in mind was the One Child Policy initiated in 1979 as China made its first national directive towards family planning to control the excess growth in its population. The world, especially those in the West, was aghast! China was roundly criticised and ridiculed. The irony was that while it is acceptable for an individual to practise birth control, it is wrong as a state policy in an otherwise populous and poor country facing starvation from uncontrolled population explosion. This moral argument can go on and on. Yet the key question, which the critics found hard, and indeed failed to answer was: how can you keep a massively growing population from hunger and famines in an otherwise poor country whose natural resources are limited without total reliance on other nations for imports of food and daily essentials at prices which are unaffordable? Will the constant reliance of food imports for a country with a huge population threaten its stability or even survival? If there was no effective population control policy in China then, it was entirely possible and probable that agricultural production would not meet the demands. What then? Would it mean an increase in infant and maternal mortality rate, or worse still, would it mean more and more abandoned infants, as happened in China during the turbulent years of the 19th Century and early 20th Century? I believe the answers to these questions are self-evident. It must also be pointed out that as China becomes more economically advanced and self-sufficient, and as its population gets older, the One Child Policy was abandoned in 2015. What was once the solution when the country was poor may not be necessary or appropriate when the country is generally better off. It is right that when the facts and the needs are different, policy adjustments are made accordingly. Policies are made for long-term progress, and not short-term gain, and too rigid a policy may have the same effect as a straitjacket.

In recent years, the criticisms of China have become much more widespread and noticeable based not just on a clash of ideology like in the past when China was poor but more based on a perceived, groundless, and imaginary threat posed by China. So the rise of China is now seen as an imminent threat from China! I personally prefer the term the 'Peaceful Renaissance of China', as I think the latter term is better tuned into the psyche of the majority of the Chinese people, given the long and non-offensive nature of its civilisation. These unfair criticisms and allegations can vary from China's territorial aggression, expansion of its defensive capabilities, its quest for new trades (The Belt and Road Initiative) to even the One Country Two Systems model for Hong Kong. Faced with these various negative comments from time to time, especially on policies which China regards as domestic issues, China defends itself on the principle of the right of any sovereign country to set its own domestic policies. In this respect, China also avoids commenting on the domestic policies of other sovereign countries.

Other countries value sovereignty too. The people of the UK voted in a referendum in 2016 to leave the European Union (EU) by a margin of 52% to 48% of the popular votes. This is now known as Brexit. One of the main arguments put forward by the advocates of the leavers was that the UK wishes to regain its sovereignty. The UK joined the EEC (the European Economic Community), then an economic model known as the Common Market, in 1973. The EEC then changed to the present model of EU (European Union) in 1993 when it changed from an economic union towards a more political union, marked significantly by a single currency called the Euro. Thus, over the ensuing 26 years, the British people and politicians feel their sovereignty in determining national policies was gradually eroded and that their right to determine the UK's own national policy was often deterred by the EU. In other words, the UK sovereignty was compromised. This led to the referendum result in 2016 in deciding to leave the EU, thus regaining sovereignty. The irony here is that when China tries to defend its domestic policy as a matter of sovereignty, there are still criticisms and yet when the UK tries to regain, not defend, its sovereignty, hardly anyone in the international community seemed to say a harsh word in criticising the UK except perhaps expression of profound regret by some EU members.

One absurd criticism is the breaching of cybersecurity, called hacking, which some point out is more common in China and even actively state sponsored. It must be argued that hacking can happen in any country. It can be initiated by anyone with mischief and ill intentions, only skills and determination are needed and the impact can be felt across national boundaries. Therefore, one can never say that the breaching of cybersecurity is specific or more prevalent in a particular country. In fact, whether someone has succeeded in hacking or not depends on how lucky the hacker is and how long the hacker manages to stay away from being caught. Modern tracking technology is such that those who do the hacking will almost invariably get caught. It matters not which country the hacker is from or where the hacking is perpetuated. In other words, breaching cybersecurity is not country specific. A brief check on the news will show that hacking can come from anywhere in the world. No one has ever proven that hacking is more common in one country than another and everyone knows that hacking can happen anytime and anywhere.

National Trauma from Late Qing Dynasty

To understand why China uses sovereignty as its legitimate defence, one must take a look at the recent history of China. The seminal starting point would be the Opium War (1839-1842) when the British Empire was at the peak of its power. Britain at the time was a seafaring, all-conquering, assertive, aggressive, and confident trading nation constantly looking for new trades and markets, while the Qing Dynasty was inexorably starting its decline after years of prosperity. Britain was then well aware of its naval power, unmatched anywhere else at the time, while the Qing Dynasty was painfully unaware of its own inadequacies and consistent failings. The Qing Dynasty started its reign in 1636 after the Manchu Clan Aisin Gioro in Manchuria (Northeast China) invaded China successfully. Indeed, the Qing

Dynasty was both powerful and successful in the first 200 years of its rule and just like other empires in history, it started to get overstretched. It slowly descended into a misguided and painfully inward-looking, self-serving nation. It failed miserably to appreciate that other nations in Western Europe had all, without fail, overtaken China, especially in the eras of the Industrial Revolutions. Moreover, the Qing Dynasty was exhausted, running out of steam, after its crushing of the Taiping Rebellion (1850-1864) and Boxer Rebellion (1899-1901). No major country in the history of the world could endure two major internal rebellions in such a short period of time while almost simultaneously facing multiple and concerted invasions from foreign powers. In its exhaustion, the Qing Dynasty's refusal and inability to engage with the others was in sharp contrast to the British Empire, which excelled in the art of diplomacy backed up by military power.

The Opium War was started by Britain to protect its economic interests, based essentially on its lucrative export of opium from India, then also a colony of the British Empire, to China. Since its introduction into China, 10 million Chinese were addicted within a year. The Qing administration had no choice but to impound and ban opium trade in Guangdong, which was the main province where opium was introduced. No country in the world, past and present, can tolerate an imported problem of that scale. Morally speaking, one must question the ethics of exporting a known addictive poison from one country to another for the sole purpose of monetary gains. The cost of growing the opium was low, the region of growing the opium not far, and yet the profit was unimaginatively huge. The Qing army was no match to the naval power of Britain. The Treaty of Nanking was the result and the island of Hong Kong was ceded to Britain in 1842. It is inconceivable in modern days that one country will declare war on another just because the latter prohibits a hugely profitable import!

This Opium War, its origin and its impact, left a long-lasting, almost irremovable feeling of trauma in the minds of all Chinese. It was indeed a very dark moment in the history of China. There then followed an almost irreversible, painful, and prolonged period, stretching over decades, of national humiliation inflicted on China. Worse still, the humiliation was inflicted not by one nation, but by a collection of rich nations, greedily hungry for land, for natural resources, and cheap labour. Every one of them was knocking at the gates for access to the markets in China, even gate crashing with military force when necessary. Their approach was always from the coast, the South China Sea and East China Sea, where most of the more prosperous cities in China were located. Japan, at the time the most modern country in Asia, also had a long-standing ambition for extra land mass in China. Japan started its invasion using Northeast China as a spearhead in Manchuria. China was being invaded from multiple fronts and fought on multiple fronts, which China was singularly ill-prepared for, from the South Coast to the East Coast to the Northeast Peninsula. In its previous long history, China was invaded mainly from land routes from the North or from the West, hence the building of the Great Wall, to keep the land-based invaders out. China had not been invaded or attacked from the seas, and had no naval expertise, thus not capable of defence against sea-based attacks.

Even though I was born in Shanghai, it was not until I reached adulthood in Hong Kong that I found out that I was born in what was known as the French Concession part of Shanghai. Shanghai has always been regarded as the most cosmopolitan and prosperous city in China. Aggression from the West was dealt with by acquiescence with the West, and major territorial concessions to foreign powers were made. Shanghai, as the most advanced city in China then, was divided into self-governing sectors by the foreign powers, with the French Concession seen as the most desirable part to live in Shanghai! So, in short, China has lost its sovereignty to govern Shanghai, one of its most cosmopolitan cities. These concessions were part of the Shanghai International Settlement in 1863, as a direct result of the defeat of China by various nations from the West. It happened because China was then demonstrably perceived as politically weak, industrially backwards, and everything, including its land mass, was ripe for grabbing.

Therefore, from the start of the decline of the late Qing Dynasty, many Chinese would regard the period, from the mid-19th century to the mid-20th century, as the Century of Humiliation. This period also coincided with the peak of the imperialistic and colonial powers from Europe which began a period of aggressive colonisation in the Far East and Africa, trading in cheap labour and raw materials and then trading out finished, polished products at a significant profit. Ironically, these were also the same nations that at the same time preached the merits of enlightenment of humanity. This Enlightenment period is regarded by some as the true initiator of liberty and the glorious chapters in Western European history. Yet it can hardly be seen as anything remotely enlightening when Europe spread its claws on China and Africa. Nothing can better describe the cliché: "History is an exercise in public relations for the victor, and is written by the victors and for the victors."

The Qing emperors and most notoriously the Empress Dowager undoubtedly made some strategic errors through their misplaced and ignorant self-deceiving grandiose ideas. Empress Dowager was even thought to have preferred to squeeze the last of the Qing's monetary reserve in building a summer palace instead of strengthening the national defence. Delusions of such grandeur played right into the hands of the invading nations which carried out untold brutalities, suffering, and imposed inequalities for the Chinese people.

The National Strife for Revival

The seeds were then sown, the May 4 Movement followed. This marked a key milestone event in modern Chinese history. It was a sort of wake-up call before it was too late. This was a historic moment for national awakening for self-reflection, and for an absolute need for self-determination and independence, free from outside influence. The movement was mainly carried out through mass but peaceful demonstrations by university students, mostly from Peking University. It called for an anti-imperialist national revival, for national sovereignty, for national technological modernisation, and political reforms. The Post World War 1 Treaty of Versailles was signed in 1919. And, as happened in every war throughout history, the powerful and victorious countries carved up their gains. In the Treaty of Versailles, the national interests and the needs of China were ignored while huge advantages, politically and territorially, were granted and conceded to neighbouring countries such as Russia and Japan. This blatant disregard of China's national interests and needs gave the May 4 Movement an extra dimension, momentum and the significance it needed. In fact, the May 4 Movement in a broader sense refers to the period from 1915-1921, known also as the New Culture Movement. The spirit of the May 4 Movement in calling for national renewal was forever formed and rooted in the national mindset, remembered and celebrated with pride by the Chinese people since as a marker for the determination of China for self-determination, reforms, national revival, and independence.

It was also at this time of the New Culture Movement that the various modern political ideologies, previously unheard of in the dynastic rules in China, were introduced into the country. Isms such as communism, socialism, capitalism were learned, openly discussed and widely debated by students and intellectuals. The Confucius philosophy, which has dominated the Chinese civilisation for thousands of years, has passed its sell-by date. Among all these ideologies, one issue did stand up clearly for the Chinese people, and that was the absolute need for national sovereignty. Ideologies may differ, the means may differ, but the ultimate aim remains unshakeable. Times of humiliation and suffering had gone on long enough. It was high time to stand up, to be independent and never to be interfered with again. The Century of Humiliation was such a recent, unique, and shameful chapter in the 5,000 year history of China. It shook the Chinese to the core, so much so that it will never be allowed to happen again. This is a national determination agreed by all Chinese, regardless of political inclination.

With this background in setting the scene, it is therefore entirely natural and understandable why the concept of sovereignty plays such a dominant role in the minds of the Chinese people and occupies such an important part in dealing with the critics of its national policies. In international diplomacy, other nation states should at least try to understand China's view of its sovereignty and its uncompromising position on this. Trade negotiations, yes, climate change negotiations, yes, full participation in the United Nations, yes, international help and aid, yes, diplomatic exchanges, yes. But interference in its sovereignty and its independence in setting up domestic and economic policy, no. This concept of sovereignty should be applicable to all nation states, big or small. For me personally, as I have mentioned previously, it is equally illuminating to recall one brief moment that in 2016, during the very heated national debate on the national referendum in the UK in remaining or leaving the European Union (EU), I remember, as clear as daylight, that one of the key advocates, in pushing to leave, stated in the UK parliament that the main reason he advocated strongly and passionately to leave was that he wanted to restore sovereignty back to the UK! So, even the UK, with its glorious colonial past, wanted to leave the EU to restore its sovereignty. It is therefore not surprising that unwarranted or unsolicited comments on China, especially those on the policies of the state, are often viewed as undermining state sovereignty. Nothing can galvanise the Chinese people more, through the prism of recent history of humiliation, than the concept of sovereignty. Furthermore, this is not seen by most people in China as an expression of narrow-minded nationalism, as some in the West would say, but really it is a matter of self-pride in the collective determination to chart their own independent national directions for the future. In the Chinese mindset, nationalism is neither narrow-minded nor fervent. It has the important connotation of the unity of the nation, restoration of the self-respect of the people and national revival. As the philosopher and political theorist Yoram Hazony highlighted in his book *The Virtue of Nationalism*: Nationalism is not some unfathomable political illness that periodically takes over countries for no good reason and to no good end, as some in the West seem to suggest. It is a principled standpoint that regards the world as governed best when nations are able to chart their own independent course, cultivating their own traditions and pursuing their own interests without interference. This is opposed to imperialism, which argues and seeks to bring peace and prosperity to the world by uniting mankind, as much as possible, under a single political regime. In other words, there is nothing wrong with nationalism. Most people in most countries are nationalistic but if the world has a single order, then this order, while claiming to bring peace and prosperity, is intrinsically imperialistic in nature.

The National Psyche

I would like to suggest that the core psyche of the Chinese people is primarily patriotic and nationalistic, but not expansionistic, certainly not imperialistic. On the point of China not being an expansionist, there needs to be further discussion and clarification. The starting point should be the Qin Dynasty in 221 BCE, now universally and historically agreed as the beginning of China being a unified state, shortly after the Warring States were defeated by Emperor Qin. The Great Wall of China was then built, at huge expense, with the sole purpose of defending China from outside invasions at its northern border. The strategic aim in defence was further reinforced 1,500 years later in the Ming Dynasty, which built further extensions and linked up the Great Wall of China. So the aim of this Great Wall, a UNESCO world heritage site, was primarily defensive in nature. Furthermore, from the time of the Qin Dynasty to the end of the Yuan Dynasty, stretching over a period of just under 1,600 years, there were only two major events when China appeared to be expanding and venturing far. One was by Genghis Khan during the Mongol Empire when the Eurasia landmass was almost exclusively conquered by the Mongols (1206-1294), reaching as far as present day Western Europe. But this Empire was very short-lived with minimal impact on the other cultures and certainly the word colonisation was hardly ever used to describe this short expansion. The other major event occurred around 200 years later, during the Ming Dynasty when a eunuch named Zheng He was commissioned by the Ming Emperor to lead a vast maritime expedition from the East China Sea, sailing south-westerly, all the way as far as the African Continent. There were, remarkably, no less than seven major voyages from 1405-1433 and yet there were no significant documented records of these voyages converting indigenous people and changing their local culture into colonies or the voyagers behaving like aggressors. Fighting and blood shed there might have been and perhaps unavoidable, but certainly there were no attempts to colonise. Furthermore, these two events, one land expansion and one sea adventurism to reach far and beyond, lasted only a very short period, and thus can best be regarded as a blip or even aberration in the dynastic history of China. These events were also regarded by most historians as having minimal impact politically, territorially, and culturally on other nations. They certainly did not lead to colonisation. This is in sharp contrast to the discovery of the New World in 1492 by Christopher Columbus, a historic event which opened the New World for conquest and permanent European colonisation of the two Americas.

Currently, two thirds of the 1.4 billion Chinese people experience uninterrupted rising living standards, peace, and progress since the end of the Cultural Revolution in 1976. The Chinese people value these above all else. The last and only major war China was engaged in was the Korean War from 1950-53. There were also the two military conflicts, one with India in 1962, and the other with Vietnam in 1979. The latter two regional conflicts lasted just about a month and can rightly be regarded as local military skirmishes around borders, hardly an international conflict of significance. There was no territorial dispute afterwards and ceasefire was rapidly arranged. The People's Republic of China entered the UN in 1971 and became one of the five permanent members of its Security Council. Since the reform and opening-up in China, initiated from 1979, it has not gone into any war. China is also now the second largest funder of the UN and the UN peacekeeping programme, contributing 2,500 peacekeepers, more than all the other permanent members of the Security Council combined. Between 2000 and 2018, it supported 182 of the 190 Security Council resolutions imposing sanctions on nations which seemed to have violated international rules or norms. China is therefore primarily nationalist in its global outlook and where internationalist multilateral issues are concerned, the main venue for China in voicing its views and opinions is through the UN. Currently, China does send its people all over the world, but these are engineers, manual workers, road/rail builders, and software designers. There are no Chinese soldiers stationed overseas, let alone military hardware. This outlook also makes it understandable why China, in carrying out its diplomatic policies, always emphasises respect for the other nation's sovereignty and right to determine its internal policies. Advice and opinions can be given but should never be imposed. Diplomacy is carried out bilaterally, multilaterally, or through the UN.

Benevolence from the West

With all the turmoil and trauma, brought about by the interaction between China and the West, it has to be recognised that there were benefits brought into China from the Western powers too. The years of humiliation not only compelled China into appreciating the might of the West and the need to learn its model of economic development and technological prowess, it also really gave China an opportunity to experience the tremendous humanitarian work of the missionaries from the West. There were very good deeds, not based on political power, gunboats, or territorial possessions by other nations, but based on the faith of the missionaries and the teachings of religion, emphasising hope, faith, and love for each other. These were the three key elements in providing some hope and some intellectual enlightening for the poor people. The missionaries not only preached their religions, but also carried out, with selfless dedication, compassion, and steadfastness, numerous acts of charities in setting up schools, clinics for public healthcare, orphanages for abandoned children, in looking after the sick in hospitals, in providing shelter and food for the homeless. Such acts of universal kindness were often carried out in extremely poor and hostile conditions. In fact, it was during these very difficult times in China, from the time of the Opium War, that Western medicine was significantly introduced and practised by the missionaries. These must not be forgotten or ignored either. These missionaries were primarily Christians, and mostly from the Catholic Church. Throughout China's history, the dominant religion was Buddhism, introduced from India during the early Tang Dynasty. Even though there was evidence suggesting that Christianity was brought into China much earlier on, it had never taken root. It was not until the 19th century that the missionaries were active participants in helping the poor, the sick, the homeless, and the starved. One can imagine the challenges these missionaries faced in keeping their faith and in helping the Chinese. Their good work left me with a lasting and unforgettable impression. To this day, their good deeds were indelible in Hong Kong, and if one looks or asks around, one would soon find out that some of the finest schools in Hong Kong were started by these missionaries.

CHAPTER 6

Technology Catch Up and Trend Settings in 21st-Century China

It is very noticeable, also widely reported in the international press, more so in the last 10 years, the significant progress that China has made in striving to change from a low-cost manufacturing-based economy to a diversified, technology-driven, service-driven economy. This shift in economic direction in moving up the value chain is the stated national policy in steering the country into the next phase of its economic development. The areas here in particular refer to digital communication (5G), artificial intelligence, big data, supercomputers, and blockchains. Other major areas of development include infrastructure projects such as the high-speed trains and rail tracks, clean and renewable energy, environmental protection, biotechnology, and cutting-edge pharmaceutical production of new drugs.

China missed the First Industrial Revolution (the age of the steam engine) and the Second Industrial Revolution (the age of steel, machinery, and electricity). Missing out on these key developments was seen by many as one of the major reasons for the Century of Humiliation. Other countries in the West capitalised on these two revolutions to propel their countries into the modern age just when China was becoming more inward-looking with a sclerotic and tired dynasty, governing a vast country which was primarily still a labour-dependent agricultural society, thus invariably fell prey to the colonial ambitions of the West. Having experienced the consequences of missing out on these technological advances, China is not about to miss out again. Indeed, China is already a key player in the Third Industrial Revolution (the age of digitalisation) and aspires to be one of the leaders in the Fourth Industrial Revolution (the age of 5G, artificial intelligence, genomics, big data, and blockchains).

The main difference between the First/Second Industrial Revolutions and the Third/Fourth Industrial Revolutions is that the former was based on cheap raw materials and cheap imported labour such as slavery, plus the mass production of goods through the use of machines, backed up by new, modern management models with the support of the government or the private banking system to provide capital within an established legal framework. These management models included accounting, establishing contractual agreements, setting of production and sales targets based on the assessment of market needs. The Third and Fourth Industrial Revolutions, by contrast, primarily depend on human intellect and mathematical principles. Countries like China and India have these in abundance because of their vast population base and traditional strength in mathematics, and so progress in these new areas is likely to continue to improve for many years to come. The playing field is therefore now more level and is relatively independent of raw materials supply from other sources.

In this new world, there is also less need for traditional sources of energy such as petrol. Petrol was once regarded for decades as the Black Gold, yet its price has hardly moved up, taking inflation into account, in the last 20 years. This is in sharp contrast compared to the oil crisis in the 1970s, when the doomsayers told us the world would run out of energy and Saudi Arabia would buy up everything there was to buy! The rapid changes in technology suggest that the Black Gold is no longer the engine of growth and prosperity, but rather technological advances and the Fourth Industrial Revolution will be the new gold, they are ubiquitous, invisible though they may be!

The Upsides of Techno-Advance

China, along with India, have the unique advantage of having a big enough critical population mass for these new technology advances to be studied, explored, tested, digitalised, and 'datarised', again and again while constantly improving their practical experience and applications, to the extent that some of these advances are already being exported abroad. These technology advances were initially privately funded, and, in some cases, state aided through either light regulation or financial backup such as tax incentives. The capital required for these was often regarded as a start-up for long-term investments for the future rather than as short-term speculative investments where returns such as dividends or capital gains are counted by investors almost daily. In China, this model of private/state collaboration is known as Socialism with Chinese Characteristics, as first coined by Deng Xiaoping. In contrast, in Silicon Valley, now viewed as the Mecca of new technology, the funding for any developments (known as upstarts) is primarily by private equity known as venture capital. The Chinese model, while undoubtedly successful in propelling China into the modern era, does have its critics, be it justified or not. The main criticism, as widely reported in some circles in the West, is that the Chinese model is state sponsored, which is not true, and not private equity sponsored, therefore citing these as unfair trade practices. Some critics even alleged that these upstarts in China often disregard or may even have been involved in theft of intellectual properties from other countries. I personally have no wish to elaborate further on this controversial debate. It can be a political hot potato, depending on which view one adopts. I would only venture to offer a personal view on the experience and journey of another very successful country.

Right after World War II, Japan was in ruins. Thereafter, with the ingenuity of its own people, and with the support from the West, mainly the USA, Japan was able to achieve outstanding economic success over the ensuing 20 years and held its place, until recent years, as the second biggest economy of the world. Japan now boasts global brands such as Sony, Olympus, Panasonic, Nikon, Toyota etc. All these household names were roundly criticised in their earlier stages of development. In the 1950s and 1960s, they were seen as cheap copycats too but who is to say there were then no issues or debates on intellectual property? These products were being sold and branded as cheap alternatives and inferior products compared to the West. The Japanese cars were not as well engineered as the German cars and were not as comfortable as the petrol-guzzling American cars, but they were cheap nonetheless. Their televisions and cameras were not as advanced as the European or the American models. Being cheap was the only thing that they had. Yet, before long, these Japanese brands and conglomerates were so successful, so admired, so world dominating that their models were copied by the rest of the world. They even started to pursue overseas acquisitions, especially in the USA. I can even remember then how the big three car manufacturers in Detroit pointed their fingers at the Japanese car imports on how they were engaged in unfair trade practices and how they were stealing jobs away from the USA. In one issue of the weekly *Time Magazine* in the 1970s, the headline was: "Is Japan taking over corporate America?" A far-fetched and overblown headline indeed. In its heydays, the Toyota car company was copied not only for the production of vehicles, but also for its famous management model called Lean Six Sigma (*Kaizen* in Japanese, meaning continued improvement) and just-in-time delivery (the predecessor of logistics). Even though it was the US company Motorola which introduced this management model, it was the Japanese company who brought this into global prominence. Sony came up with the ground-breaking Walkman. Yet, advances in one country can be turned around, for reasons of political ideology and rhetoric, to accusations of theft of intellectual property in another country in different eras and different times! The irony is, looking back now, that exactly the same allegations of theft of intellectual property and unfair trading practices were levied against Japan in the 1970s and 1980s at the height of Japan's economic boom. There were even books written about it with inflammatory titles such as *The Coming War with Japan*! Over dramatisation and scaremongering were happening then and are perhaps happening now.

A Metaphor

I often think of the story of a poor but determined child, not quite well-educated, but by sheer determination was admitted to a school for the elite. He was utterly taken in by the wonderful surroundings and all the smart, well-spoken, smartly dressed school mates. In order to be like them, he buckled down to work hard, learn hard with a will power that few could match, despite the occasional bullying by some. Day in and day out he tried hard, hoping that one day he would be as successful as the smart lads, so he could take care of the brothers and sisters he has at home. He was very humble. He did his homework diligently and at school he kept asking his teachers and seniors to guide him, learning from them as his role models. Initially he struggled, his work was slightly sloppy, and he was teased, ridiculed, and even looked down upon by others at school. He kept his head down but his spirits were never down. Gradually he started to improve. At the graduation ceremony, he came top of the class, much to the surprise of teachers and the other smart students, some of whom jealously sneered at him and even suspected him of cheating at the examinations, since a boy of that background, so ignorant initially, so out of place, so different in his demeanour, could not have come up with such good grades.

Historically, as mentioned in the previous chapter, this massive effort in China for a national technology catch up has its seeds first sown in the May 4 Movement in 1919. This movement was a milestone in modern Chinese history as it played a key part in changing the Chinese psyche from an inward-looking one to an outward-looking one, with determination and enthusiasm to learn from the others. Regrettably, the subsequent civil wars put paid to these national aspirations, as there was no national unity and therefore no national strategy for years and years. Each local power (known as warlords) was mainly interested in clinging to its territorial power. Now, 100 years later, the achievement of these techno-aspirations is within sight. In China, the move into the modern techno age is well and truly established.

The following is what I see as the result of integrating technology and its application to daily life in China. Everywhere I go, I can see most working men no longer carry briefcases, their backpacks no longer have laptops but flasks for water, towels or umbrellas, and ladies don't carry handbags. Nearly all of them, from all walks of life, carry a smartphone (a more appropriate term would be a mobile portable device), in which there are so many new apps. These apps are so convenient, fast, reliable, versatile, and multifunctional that they actually can serve as a camera, a video or sound recorder, a payment device, a personal organiser, an e-reader, a music player, and an information centre, including GPS. Talking on the phone is just but one of its many functions. In fact, if one observes the users closely, one can easily notice that more time is now spent on looking and tapping on the screen than talking on the phone. When going to tourist hot spots, one does not see people with long lens bulky cameras or compact cameras but selfie sticks with smartphones. Of course, it is also truly a 24/7 service in the palm of your hand for daily needs such as checking when the bus will be arriving, what food or goods to order, booking a cinema ticket and even looking at your own blood tests done a day before in a hospital. I have personally witnessed, on a day-to-day basis, how my Chinese colleagues use these apps with such consummate skills. When I am back in the UK, which most would agree is also fairly techno savvy, I also see people using their phones for a variety of purposes, but nowhere near as widely as in China. No wonder one of the key areas of research these days for these smart devices is on how to prolong the battery life, just like having a modern car whose kilometres per litre of petrol is higher and higher, or for an electric car in the future which will have batteries lasting longer, covering more and more kilometres, once fully charged. We will all be dependent, as is obvious these days, on these smart devices. Furthermore, the advance in general logistics in integrating the online-to-offline (O2O) services is so efficient in China that anything we order online not only is delivered fast to our doorstep, but every step in its delivery is now trackable. This is now a social phenomenon in daily life, where I often see people on scooters delivering goods and hot meals. In fact, the success and the convenience of this O2O service are seen by many as one of the reasons for the demise of the shopping malls. I use smart phones and the O2O as simple examples to demonstrate Chinese prowess in using technology, as nowhere else have I witnessed these used as widely and as smartly as in China. China has now truly emerged as a main provider of these mobile devices as well as the users of the devices. The Chinese welcome and embrace new gadgets and this will in turn motivate greater incentive for the gadget providers to innovate.

China's Homegrown Techno Giants

The current global big techno firms such as Facebook, Google, Amazon, Apple, broadly called the Silicon Valley phenomenon, are already beginning to be matched in China with similar brands. These are Alibaba (e-commerce), Baidu (Google-like search engine in China), Tencent (an IT software company) and its WeChat (regarded in China as app of all apps), Huawei (a telecommunications equipment supplier and a mobile phone provider), DJI (Da Jian Innovation, pioneering in drones). Just like the global giants, these Chinese giants have been shown to be equally innovative. Their services and products are just as reliable, durable, sustainable, and user-friendly. On top of that, they are cheaper, backed up not only by a huge domestic market, but also a market which is one of the most competitive in the world, and estimated to boast the biggest middle class in human history. In terms of going global, some of these products are already thriving in the export markets.

So, the evolution from an agriculture-based in the past to a manufacturing-based economy in the recent past to a service-based, knowledge-based, technology-based economy presently is already unfolding right in front of our eyes. This trend is gaining momentum. The speed of the progress is such that the time gap between the first two industrial revolutions was roughly 70 years while the time gap between the last two industrial revolutions is estimated to be roughly 20 years only. One has to keep running just to keep still. The national aspiration of technology catching up as expressed by the May 4 Movement 100 years ago has now become achievable realities in China.

Two areas need special mention to illustrate the point of the huge impact these advances have on the lives of ordinary Chinese. I recalled that it was about two years ago when I saw a special report by the British Broadcasting Corporation (BBC) on how China was moving ahead to be the first country to progress successfully to a cash-free society. I myself do not understand the ultimate modern day application of Bitcoin but I do appreciate the need for cash-free transactions which traditionally use credit or debit card as a form of payment with a PIN (personal identification number) and authorisation process, with each transaction still needing a major clearing bank to back it up. So in our own lives, because we are used to using cards to replace cash, all of us will end up carrying multiple cards, loyalty cards, membership cards, and now most people carry a wallet full of cards, certainly mine does. And so, on reading that BBC report, I started to pay attention to this and indeed, it became so obvious that 90% of the day-to-day transactions in China are now cash free or card free, based on the WeChat or Alipay app mentioned previously. The transactions can vary from paying for hospital consultation fees, to paying for a taxi ride, to ordering food or even shopping for either groceries or a single can of soda. I was very impressed with this, not least because I have found it very difficult to carry Chinese cash (known as *renminbi* or RMB in short) with me due to its great variation in the paper value, colours, and coins. So, a cash-free society offers not only convenience and an electronic record, but also contributes to a greener environment. I was so astounded when a few years ago I went to a remote village in China and noticed that the small corner shop was selling food via cash-free transaction, and the customers all paid their bills with a smartphone. Of course, this trend is now beginning to be noticed in other countries too but nowhere as widespread and common as in China. It is almost like standard practice! The BBC was absolutely right!

The other area to mention is in my own field of medicine. I have personal experience in noting the advances in cutting-edge treatment, such as cellular immunotherapy or targeted therapy in tackling cancers and other diseases, which are being developed in China. There is also the early, embryonic emergence of what an internet hospital will be like. There is an upstart in China called We Doctor Holdings, a technology-enabled healthcare consultation IT company which offers a platform integrating government, hospitals, doctors, pharmaceuticals, and local pharmacies. This is a new concept of an ecosystem in healthcare, boasting a forum with 2,700 hospitals, 220,000 doctors, 15,000 pharmacies and 27 million monthly users, a kind of early prototype for an internet hospital.

China is now not only a key stakeholder and contributor in the technology world of the 21st century, more is to come from the pipeline. According to the World Intellectual Property Organisation (WIPO), China has retained its position as the world leader in patent applications, with Chinese companies and individuals responsible for 40% of all patent applications submitted in 2017. Asia has also strengthened its position as the region with most patent filings, with Asian offices receiving 65% of all applications filed in 2018 up from 50% in 2007. As a famous political commentator once pointed out, while the USA is still the leader in many areas, we are seeing what is termed the 'Rise of the Rest'. While the centre of gravity of technological advances post WWII was somewhere near mid-Atlantic, this centre of gravity may now be shifting to somewhere closer to China and India in Asia.

Worthy of special mention is progress in the developments of artificial intelligence (AI), big data, quantum computers, and 5G. AI will need well-developed algorithms, superfast real-time computing of comprehensive data sets, even non-specific data to generate a big and accurate assessment for a defined outcome and objective. I would guess that in the not too distant future, I will witness the practical applications of these developments in our daily lives, such as driverless cars, non-traffic light-based traffic controls, seamless transport of services and goods.

The Challenges of Techno-Advance

Ironically for the medical profession, this may also possibly make being a medical doctor the new sunset profession, just like it is foreseeable that seeking accounting or legal advice may be a thing of the past (one can do most of this on the net). The new world will ultimately seek to replace these professional services. As a result, people always ask me how I feel about this trend or what would my advice be on entering a medical career for the younger generation. My answer to that is fairly straightforward, perhaps idealistic even. I pointed out that all technological advances, for as long as they are not abused like the atomic bombs since nuclear energy was discovered, have proved to be beneficial for the common good of mankind. An invention or a new tool is seldom wrong, but often it is the way we use or exploit it that is wrong. As for being a doctor, one thing we can trump over AI and big data is our cognitive function and our ability to empathise with patients. All the calculations, algorithms, big data, and deep learning worked out by AI and the supercomputer behind a screen cannot compete with us in our real world of sentiments, empathy, and compassion. This may be our competitive edge in this new world. So the end is not in sight and the future, at least for my profession, is still bright. The time has not come, not even on the horizon, for us to live in a world where when we need a surgical operation, we proceed to tap onto a screen or speak over a wireless speech recognition gadget, then see a robot, rather than seeing a team of professionals, such as what is happening now. If we are to have a major surgery, surgeons, anaesthetists, theatre assistants, the nurses, the post-operative physiotherapists or pharmacists are all part of a team to help us. Can AI really do all these, I wonder! And even if AI and robots can do that, would we accept that? Even the most advanced robots for a given surgical operation need well-trained doctors to steer and operate the robot. Technology can help us, but not replace us.

PART 2: ON MY WORK

CHAPTER 7

A Brief Description of Shenzhen

Shenzhen is a city north of the border from Hong Kong and the distance between them is about 27 km. In comparison, the two closest major cities in England are Manchester and Liverpool, with a distance between them of about 33 km. It takes 30 minutes from the centre of Hong Kong to get to the centre of Shenzhen by high-speed rail and about 60 minutes by car. For me, since I mainly use public transport, it takes me 90 minutes door-to-door from my home in Hong Kong to my office in Shenzhen.

Prior to 1979, Shenzhen was a little unknown fishing village with a population of just under 60,000. In 1979, the then paramount leader in China, Deng Xiaoping, launched a national economic reform and opening-up policy to be tried out in the newly created Special Economic Zones (SEZs) based on the introduction of market economy with many new initiatives including land reforms and tax changes. Shenzhen was designated as one of the SEZs.

Within a period of just 40 years, Shenzhen has changed from a fishing village with a population of 60,000 to a major megametropolis in China. The latest figure in 2017 showed that it has an estimated population of 13.7 million residents. Projections for the next five years showed that if floating populations such as temporary migrant workers are to be included, it may reach 20 million. The average age of the local population is 32, making the city boasting to have one of the youngest working populations in China. In 2017, its GDP was the third highest in China, behind Shanghai and Beijing and has overtaken Hong Kong. This is a staggering achievement, an achievement that almost defies belief and comprehension. If we wind back the time clock, and imagine ourselves to be on a group tour visiting Shenzhen some 40 years ago as a countryside village near the border with Hong Kong, would any of us even remotely imagine this village would be transformed into its present state?

How does Shenzhen Achieve this Remarkable Feat?

First, the timing. It was only a fishing village, with no history and therefore, no historical burden or luggage when it was designated as a SEZ. It could start on a clean sheet of paper. Everything could start afresh, develop afresh, supported by a new generation of upwardly mobile, aspiring and young population.

Then there is the entrepreneurial and far-sighted local government which, with the staunch support of the central government, proceeded to set up a string of policies in tax and land reforms to attract foreign direct investments, mainly from neighbouring Hong Kong. In attracting these foreign direct investments inwards, the local government also started a very comprehensive infrastructure expansion programme including a very efficient transport system consisting of a new international airport, new high-speed train system, an extensive local underground system, and other public transport such as buses and taxis. At the same time, more land was made available for setting up factories, commercial, and residential buildings.

The third reason for its success is its proximity to Hong Kong, another modern day metropolis, which can then provide and import into Shenzhen modern know-how of management, investments, and accounting practices in setting up factories, advising on banking practices, and providing an outlet to a global network for exportable products made in Shenzhen. It has often been said that Shenzhen would not be what it is today without Hong Kong and equally Hong Kong cannot be what it is today without Shenzhen. The two cities are made to fit into each other's needs. Over the subsequent years since 1979, the transfer of this know-how transformed Shenzhen into a very outward and forward-looking city, welcoming not only Hong Kong-based investments but also overseas investments by major multinationals, especially in the production and assembly of world-famous brands in the fashion, television, and mobile phone industries. Just like Hong Kong, Shenzhen is now a thriving and vibrant city.

Initially, the economic emphasis was based on the availability of low paid and young workers recruited from all over the country to work in newly set up factories mainly for manufacturing products for export such as garments, watches, electronic gadgets, shoes, toys, furniture, and a wide variety of consumer products. The joke being that, you name it, Shenzhen makes it. It is estimated that around 30% of the world's manufactured products are now made in China, the name 'Factory of the World' is used as a label to mark the manufacturing prowess of China and Shenzhen is one of the main manufacturing hubs in the country. These products are not only cheap because of the low labour and start-up costs but their quality and durability are equally good. The production of the Apple iPhones in Shenzhen is but one example. Much has been said about equally cheap labour costs in other Asian countries, such as Vietnam and Cambodia, as alternative manufacturing bases, but it is now widely recognised that China still arguably offers the best skilled labour force which produces good quality and durable products. This is a result of the cumulative experience of not only in the manufacturing processes but also in logistic areas such as transport, distribution, and sourcing as well. This skilled labour force and the whole chain of logistics are now about to move to a higher level.

Of course, the visionary local Shenzhen government is not about to rest on its laurels and be content with using its manufacturing success as the basis for continued economic strength. It aims for a more dynamic and modern economy. So the local government started in the early 2000s the move towards making high-end products and developing services and modern, smokeless industries such as finance, insurance, telecommunications, information technology, and bioengineering. It is truly amazing to witness that, in a short span of 10 years, the city has made remarkable progress in completely transforming its economic model from low-cost manufacturing to high-end services which require a much higher start-up capital but powered on by a new generation of entrepreneurs consisting of skilled young workers, software engineers, and marketing experts. And noticeably too, Shenzhen is particularly strong in areas where global competition is relentlessly fierce, such as tablets, smartphones, and software developments. Shenzhen now boasts to house the headquarters of the giant and global telecommunications supplier Huawei, the software company Tencent, whose WeChat is now regarded as a better version of Facebook in China, Da Jian Innovation, which is known for its world-leading drone development, plus other service giants such as Ping An Insurance, the biggest insurance company in China, and the

BGI group, the world's biggest genomic sequencing laboratory. The city is now ranked as one of the top five cities in China with an international reputation. In fact, the travel guide Lonely Planet ranked Shenzhen second as one of the top 10 must-see cities in the world in 2019 after Copenhagen in Denmark. It described Shenzhen as follows: "Hyper modern architecture, innovative environmental practices and a slew of new design openings, all connected to neighbouring Hong Kong by high-speed rail". The aspiration now is to make Shenzhen in the near future the Silicon Valley of the East.

The Need for Concurrent Infrastructure Expansion

This rapid economic development cannot proceed without a concurrent development of other important service areas such as transport, housing, education, medical services, and environmental protection, since the official estimate is that within five years from 2017, the Shenzhen resident population may reach 20 million. Of far more importance is the announcement by the State Council in February 2019 that there will be the creation of the Guangdong-Hong Kong-Macao Greater Bay Area (GBA). All the cities within this vast area in the province of Guangdong will be linked up by roads, bridges, and high-speed rails and airport. All the manufacturing and services industries will be linked up with each area developing into a leading role where it can excel, such as Shenzhen will be a leading IT centre while Hong Kong will be a leading financial centre. This vast area will be the engine for growth for the new sunrise industries, the centre of learning and knowledge for education and medical services including new drug developments in southern China.

It is with this vision that the concept for our hospital Hong Kong

University Shenzhen Hospital (HKU SZH) was conceived, designed, and built. Back in 2008, the Shenzhen government decided that to support the rapid growth of the population, expansion in both hospital and education services were needed. Prior to that, where medical services were concerned, many patients chose to go to Guangzhou for diagnosis and treatment (a two-hour car drive up north on a good day) especially for major diseases like cancers. The expansion of hospital services by the government included a massive plan for building new hospitals, each hospital being linked with a university institution. In this programme, HKU SZH was the first one off the block, opened in July 2012. The hospital was also chosen to be a major reform hospital, to collaborate with and to be run by the University of Hong Kong (HKU), aiming to provide medical services in a way that is different from the traditional mainland hospitals. It is managerially run by staff employed via HKU. This was an unprecedented project. Even though HKU has never run a hospital (hospitals in Hong Kong are either run by the Hong Kong Hospital Authority, wholly funded by the Government through general taxation, or they could be privately owned), the Medical Faculty's close collaboration with its main affiliated teaching hospital, the Queen Mary Hospital (QMH) on HK Island, has made QMH the premier hospital in Asia with outstanding standards in undergraduate teaching, excellent achievements in research portfolio, and top notch modern specialist services. The aspiration of the Shenzhen government is that this new hospital, invested and owned by the Shenzhen government and run and developed by HKU, will then emerge as a similar premier hospital like Queen Mary Hospital.

CHAPTER 8

A Brief Description of HKU SZH

Chosen to be located in a newly created green and residential area, the architectural design and plan for the setting up of the Hong Kong University Shenzhen Hospital (HKU SZH) started in earnest by the Shenzhen government in the early 2000s, with a total public investment of RMB4 billion, for a hospital with a bed capacity of 2,000, covering 37,000 square metres. This HKU SZH is a modern hospital built to meet the healthcare needs of the residents but aspired to be run as a high-standard service based on an alternative model, similar to the hospitals in the West, as well as emphasising the environmental needs of the new Millennium. It opened to the public on July 1st 2012.

The management model of the hospital consists of a Board of Directors with both executive and non-executive members, chaired by the Deputy Mayor of Shenzhen. Members of the Board consist also of representatives from HKU, the Shenzhen Health Bureau, hospital staff, as well as the public.

The hospital chief executive (HCE) is appointed jointly by HKU and the Shenzhen government. He is assisted by a party secretary, who has a key role in coordinating and advising on the party and state policies at the local level. This arrangement is actually working well to align the hospital developments with that of the country. There are also several assistant HCEs. The core aims of this collaboration will focus on three main areas: clinical service excellence, teaching excellence, and research excellence, along the same model which was established in HKU and its teaching hospital Queen Mary Hospital. More specifically, there is also a focus on the following clinical areas designated as Areas of Excellence: Cardiology, Organ Transplantation, Oncology (including Bone Marrow Transplantation), Infection, Orthopaedics, IVF (In Vitro Fertilisation)/Antenatal Care.

Currently, the hospital employs about 690 full-time mainland Chinese doctors with around 20% being senior specialists (consultant or associate consultant level), 40% being middle grade specialists, and 40% being residents. These are supported by about 88 senior doctors of professorial or consultant grade and managers employed by HKU (part timers or full timers), mainly in senior clinical or administrative positions. These 88 staff are recruited from Hong Kong, the UK, the USA, Canada, and Australia.

As part of the overall mission of providing innovative models of clinical services and as a pilot of healthcare reforms in China, some major policy directions were set at the beginning as the guiding principles. These include setting up a hospital-based General Practice Department with a government-approved package charge, the establishment of a PRO (Patients Relation Office), the zero-tolerance policy to violence, the appointments booking systems, the introduction of hospital indemnity by a commercial insurance company, the prohibition of accepting red packets, the emphasis on teamwork and evidence-based medicine, clinical transparency, and open disclosure. In implementing these policies, HKU SZH also aims to achieve both international and national accreditation of its services within a five-year period. All these will be discussed in further detail in the following sections.

CHAPTER 9

Preparations for the Journey

It was March 2012 when I, with the support of my wife and son, decided to accept the offer to work at HKU SZH. The transition from one job to another is never easy, let alone a transition from a standardised and much-admired system known as the National Health Service (NHS) in the UK to working in China in which the healthcare system is still undergoing major and regular changes. It can also mean that the system can be different between the coastal metropolitan cities and the inland villages, where mythical folklore healing is still very much believed in and has been practised for generations. This is because China is not only the most populous country in the world, this massive population also has within itself diverse cultures, different dialects, and culinary traditions varying between north and south, east and west; a huge degree of heterogeneity in a sovereign country! For instance, the preferred carbohydrate intake for the south is primarily based on rice while the north is mainly noodles and buns.

So, not only do I need to prepare myself professionally as a doctor, I also need to have a working knowledge of actually living in China, especially in a modern city like Shenzhen where it does not have an indigenous population. Most of its residents are immigrants from all over the country. In other words, the city, while modern, may also be a melting pot for various diverse cultures. So, for me, there are regional traditions and cultures to understand and accept. A patient may have the same disease classifiable under the ICD (International Classification of Diseases) code but the way the patient actually deals with the disease will vary based on their own lifestyle, habits, and cultural traditions. This, in a vast country with a continuous history of more than 5,000 years, is hardly surprising.

Learning Putonghua

I knew this would turn out to be a life-changing and transformational event for me. I needed to face it with tenacity, courage, and fortitude. In order to help myself to adapt to this new life, new job, and a completely new environment, the first thing I needed to do was to be able to communicate and articulate. It was imperative that I could speak Chinese with the Chinese people, so I started to learn the national Chinese language of *putonghua* (traditionally known as mandarin). Being a Shanghai-born Chinese brought up in Hong Kong, I can only speak Cantonese (the language spoken by nearly all the local Chinese in Hong Kong), *putonghua* was something I could comprehend partly but was not a language I spoke regularly. And yet, it would be inappropriate and indeed unacceptable if I came to work in China speaking only fluent English or Cantonese. This would cause a major communication problem in talking with colleagues, patients, and their families, especially in the day-to-day practice of medicine, where misunderstanding and wrong interpretation must be avoided at all costs. A drug which sounds familiar to me in English is completely incomprehensible to me in Chinese and the use of drugs is one area that allows no room for mistakes or misunderstandings.

But *putonghua*, as I later found out, was not that difficult to learn. I told myself that practice makes perfect. Acquiring another spoken language when I can already read in Chinese is a skill definitely worth having. So, for the three months before I arrived in China, I watched CGTN (China Global Television Network) at home in the UK every evening. One hour was spent watching the news and current affairs analysis while another hour was spent watching popular TV dramas (especially the medical ones!). I gradually began to understand the reports and the dialogues. The advantages of watching these programmes were that all these have subtitles in simplified Chinese (the written Chinese I am used to is mainly the traditional form, used mainly in Hong Kong and Taiwan, while mainland China uses exclusively the simplified form). If at any point I could not follow the story, I simply pressed the pause button on the remote control and read the words in the subtitles, sometimes even rewinding the programme to learn the words again. It was very flexible. I could choose when to start watching them, as these are generally available 24 hours a day or I could even set them on recording mode. This sort of learning was quite enjoyable too as I got to know the news as well as enjoying some TV dramas. There was one medical drama series that I found particularly useful in which the hot topics in medical services in China were described and portrayed in detail, such as medical disputes, consent, complaints, its modus operandi, uniforms, and even dress codes! Even though these programmes may have used their artistic licence to dramatize the issues depicted, they were nonetheless quite authentic and relevant for my purpose. This helped me to at least begin to appreciate what lay in wait for me in China before my arrival, especially in areas related to being a doctor, but also in areas pertaining to social trends and popular culture.

In addition, I also knew that I needed real life practice in speaking *putonghua* both as a doctor and a citizen in Shenzhen. It was fortunate for me that the hospital I worked in at the time in the UK had many medically trained doctors from China doing scientific research on sponsored programmes by the Chinese or UK governments and academic institutions. They were my colleagues whom I saw on a regular basis in the department. I arranged to have dinners with them weekly, not merely to seek their advice for someone in my situation going into the unknown and unfamiliar, but also actually practising my *putonghua*, either playing a role as a patient, a doctor, or a friend. This would help me in practising and polishing my ability to chat leisurely, effortlessly for both social and professional reasons. I suspect they enjoyed the role they played in tutoring me more than they liked the food I had on offer from the local Chinese restaurant! They not only advised me, they actually encouraged me. They pointed out that it was such an unusual and unique opportunity to see someone daring enough to go in the other direction, from the West to the East. During this period of learning *putonghua*, I had lots of fun, including the many instances where my pronunciations were such a source of amusement that everyone just laughed hilariously, including myself. I am grateful for their time and effort. These are fond memories to be had.

The Dos and Don'ts

I also drew up a list of dos and don'ts. One of the major don'ts for me was not to say things like, or even think like: why do you do it this way in China, as we in the UK do it in a different way? Or, why is this drug not used here in China while it is widely used regularly in the UK? To me, this is patronising and even insulting, reflecting a conceited attitude. One must understand things before starting to ask why. Hasty judgemental opinions can often be based on prejudices and preconceived impressions and not on facts. Working with each other must involve mutual respect. In my case, it was me who decided to go to China and work as a doctor. I should not be presumptuous to form premature judgements in any way other than seeing this primarily as an opportunity for me to get to know and understand the Chinese system. In doing so, it may enable me to introduce and pioneer some changes in the hospital for the better, no matter how trivial the changes may be. I saw myself as a small but usable bridge linking both sides along the riverbanks. However tiny or short this bridge may be, it can always be of some help to some people at some time.

The other key consideration on my list was not to be too high profile, not because of humility on my part but more so on the fact that one should only say something when there is something to say. Expression of aspirations, ideals, targets are all very important and desirable but if these are repeated again and again, they may be seen as hollow talk and worse still, regurgitations. Looking back, I think it was the right approach. I was asked to do various TV and press interviews, most of which I politely declined. Besides, I am camera shy. In China, or indeed anywhere else, it should always be the deeds and the outcome that count and not the rhetoric.

One important thing on my to-do list, which may be considered to be controversial, was not to be too target-driven, especially financial targets. In China, all public hospitals are run on a yearly break-even basis where annual income should balance the spending, government subsidies will only account for about 10-15% of the annual budget. This is a system totally different from the National Health Service (NHS) in the UK, which is a system where the spending is underwritten by the government through general taxation. Had I accepted or acquiesced with this financial self-independence model, I would surely have failed, perhaps even miserably. I often tried to explain to the senior hospital managers and Shenzhen Health Bureau officials in passing that if this were indeed the target set for me, I should not have been appointed nor should I have taken up the offer. Accounting and income generation are simply not in my DNA, however hard I may try. For a new hospital like HKU SZH, credibility, reputational integrity, and patient safety should be the guiding principles, things that money can't buy and take years to achieve. They always accepted my views. I think the major reason for their acceptance is that HKU SZH was mainly invested by the Shenzhen government with the intention to create an alternative service model, including new funding reforms in healthcare, as a spark to ignite changes. Medical practitioners should see patients on clinical need and not on twisted financial considerations. If financial motive was one of the main motives for the practitioners, then there will always be an alternative for them, such as entering into the private sector, just like many other doctors in China, Hong Kong, or some in the UK do. This is not to say that financial prudence is not important, far from it, but it should not be the prime and only consideration in running a hospital. The government wished us to initiate some reforms and the first reform, in my mind, was to start with the right attitude, which the public, patients, and staff would welcome and find refreshing.

There was also a need to have a good professional relationship with my peers from mainland China working in other hospitals in Shenzhen. I knew they would all watch HKU SZH and its developments with much interest and curiosity. They were the experienced and established local leaders. Their opinions and support mattered. I may not agree with them on various issues, though more often than not, I later found out, we had more similarities than differences, which is most gratifying. I could listen and learn from them; the local way can be more practical and useful than the foreign way. I had absolutely no reason not to take their advice seriously. Collaboration should be as equally important and motivating as competition. There are more positives in the concept of collaboration while there may be more negatives in the concept of competition, medical services are not a business, therefore should not be completely based on the commercial model of competition.

I also need to appreciate our staff as our most valued asset. I did not have an existing team and had to build one from scratch. Interviews were held for each medical appointment. Because the hospital is a non-traditional hospital in many ways in its day-to-day operations and is different from the way most other hospitals are run, where there were already established terms and conditions for standard employment of staff, those staff who joined our department would need to have a spirit of adventure, just like me, coming all the way from the UK. This spirit of adventure, the feeling of camaraderie, needed to be harnessed, and would help to establish teamwork, promoting collective contributions. While I did not have extensive knowledge about the format and the language that are traditionally used in the completion of application forms for medical appointments in China and thus not very certain on how to assess accurately the merits of the applications, I did have some experience in the UK of interviewing and appointing both junior and senior medical staff. This experience helped to put me in good stead. I could make up for the shortfalls and gaps in their application forms by asking some very searching questions, or even, for some senior appointments, inviting them to visit the hospital for an informal chat, prior to the formal interview, thus allowing me to make better decisions.

CHAPTER 10

A General Discussion on Health Services in China

It is not the aim of this book to describe in detail, let alone explain, the health service provision in China. A brave attempt, however, based on personal observations, is made here.

Published data from the Organization for Economic Cooperation and Developments (OECD) in 2014 showed that China spent about 5.4% of its GDP per year on healthcare services, while the USA, which has a population one quarter of that of China, spent almost exactly three times higher at 16.9%. The US spend is the highest in the world, the equivalent figure for the UK is 9.3%, which is right in the middle of the average range of OECD. Another survey to take note of is the Commonwealth Fund International Health Policy Survey, a non-profit organisation based in New York which, consistently over the last decades, ranked the UK system among the top three. This regular survey, carried out every few years, does not include China but does include seven countries with comparable healthcare standards. These are the USA, the UK, Germany, Canada, the Netherlands, Australia, and New Zealand. The survey is based on criteria such as quality of care, efficiency, access, equity, long healthy productive lives, and health spending per capita, adjusted for purchasing power parity. For the USA, the net spend per capita was

USD7,290/year while the figure for the UK was USD2,992/year and yet the USA ranks bottom consistently in this survey, suggesting that spending the most does not necessarily lead to the best ranking when various healthcare indicators are considered. This survey does not take into account research, advances in diagnostics, genomic studies, or treatments of any specific diseases.

In a country like China, with a huge population of 1.4 billion people, of various geographic layouts, climatic patterns, diversified culture, and ethnicity invariably mean that there will be regional differences in economic developments and personal prosperity. As healthcare provision is very resource intensive, it is therefore inevitable that the standards of care, the availability, and the scope of the services provided in any given city or province are dependent both on the national and local economy.

In China, basic health insurance has been provided by the state since 2011, to cover roughly 95% of urban and rural populations. Provision of health services in China is regarded not only as state obligation by providing state insurance but also the responsibility of individuals. In recent years, there is the realisation and national acceptance that basic state-sponsored health insurance may not be comprehensive enough and yet too prohibitive in cost to be shouldered solely by the national government. A case in point, for the sake of comparison, is that in the UK, the net spend, adjusted for inflation, of the National Health Service since its inception from 1948/9 to 2014/5, has shot up from a total of GBP12 billion/year initially to about GBP135 billion/year, an increase of more than 10 times. This rate of increase has shown no sign of slowing down. In fact, the consensus view is that the rise in demand will continue to outpace the rise of inflation, thus needing more and more net increase year-on-year. The reason is simple. It is the combination of the rapid medical advances and an ageing population. This problem is universal. In China, just like many other healthcare systems, often the shortfalls or gaps are filled by co-payment by personal means. This co-payment works most of the time, especially for one-off procedures such as hip replacement or cataract operation. When it comes to dealing with complex, life-threatening diseases such as leukaemia, then it can cause many problems. New drugs are now available, but very expensive. Supportive tools such as radiological imaging, histological and genetic diagnosis are more precise but equally expensive, especially in the last 10 years.

Regional Variations in State Medical Cover

The more prosperous cities, like Shenzhen, Shanghai, or Beijing, have a more extensive local government medical insurance cover for those with major illnesses such as kidney failures, cancer, or leukaemia. This will help the local residents who have bought into this fairly generous local government scheme. However, this level of state cover can vary from city to city. This variance in the level of cover in the provision of state medical insurance in China arose as a result of the disparity of economic prosperity between regions, especially between the well-developed coastal cities and those inland cities. Because of the huge advances in medical technology and treatment, this variance is becoming a national issue. Such advances in treatment are so significant that they can even mean the emergence of a completely new, interventional-based treatment model with the aim of saving life in replacement of what was in the past a passive and reactive, hope-for-the-best treatment. For example, I can remember that when I was a very young resident working in a cardiac intensive care unit, the only treatment for a patient admitted with a heart attack (myocardial infarction) was complete bed rest for weeks while hoping the heart could slowly recover with no other complications. If complications such as heart failure or abnormal heart beats occurred, then we could only use medications to deal with them with partial success. These days, most heart attacks can be treated, under local anaesthesia, by the insertion of a stent in the coronary blood vessels to restore the circulation for the heart before permanent cardiac damage and complications set in.

Faced with this problem, the central government is already actively working on and exploring various solutions to minimise this regional variation, so that cover across the whole nation can be more equitable. The necessary prerequisite in addressing a better cover first and foremost is sustainable economic growth, which is still the national priority set by the government. I am hopeful and confident that this regional variance will become smaller as China continues to advance its economic developments.

In this modern age of advanced healthcare, affordability often equates or even ensures accessibility. This is a major issue affecting not only China but nearly all countries. It is simply impossible to match the national resources with modern healthcare demands and expectations. As our living standards improve, our expectations in areas like health and education will rise, this is typically known as the middle-class trap. Just like we are so used to using 4G or 5G mobile phones, we would not want to go back to 2G. This rising expectation of the people in seeking better, more modern healthcare is entirely understandable and needs to be managed. China has, in the last 40 years, mainly been engaging in an active economic catch up game, going through various development challenges and transformation stages. Despite the GDP of China being the second largest in the world, it is nonetheless a country with a per capita income in the upper middle range as estimated by the World Bank, lower than the other less populous countries with more mature economies, which have a per capita income in the upper range. The income per capita in China is 1/6 of that of the USA and 1/4 of that of the UK. So the state cannot afford nor should it be expected to fund comprehensively all aspects of the health services. To expect the state to bear the burden solely is unrealistic. There needs to be some acceptable form of rationing, as they do in some other countries. The Chinese people understand and indeed accept the difficulty here. This means both alternative and additional funding is needed. In addition, because of this funding gap and the increased prosperity of its people, there is therefore a growing need and potentially big market for private capital to step in to invest in commercial private health insurance in the Chinese healthcare sector. The niche in this market is mainly in non-emergency services which can be planned and which have high public demands. These include procedural services like interventional radiology or cardiac imaging, endoscopic procedures, and obstetrics services (China abandoned its One Child Policy in 2015, replacing it with a universal Two Child Policy).

The Role of Private Enterprises

China already now has all the necessary conditions required to enter into the world of maturing private medical insurance as an additional tool, not a replacement, for funding healthcare. Not only is there governmental encouragement and support for private investment in the development of commercial private health care insurance, there is also a national willingness for people to buy private medical insurance through personal means or company schemes, very similar to the US model. In addition, China has an emerging and huge well-informed middle class, an ageing population, a growing and changing economy from manufacturing economy to a service economy (we used to sell goods but now we provide service), seasoned netizens and consumers, all serving as magnets for private medical insurance for entry into this huge market. The big magnet for the big insurance conglomerates, national or international, is that this market in China will have the biggest and ever-growing middle-class population the world has ever seen. We, the middle class, are all used to buying car insurance, house insurance, and travelling insurance. All these are designed to minimise our risk when we have an accident, so we naturally would also consider private medical insurance too. It is possible to hope that with the government encouragement in private medical insurance schemes, the drain on personal resources, in the event of medical needs, can be significantly lessened.

This is already happening. In China, everywhere I look, especially in the major cities, I see major investments made by private enterprises in promoting various insurance-based health services. These investments are not only for outpatient-based medical centres, but more ambitiously, for building brand-new private hospitals too. One of the most successful and famous hospitals in Beijing is a privately run hospital which mainly specialises in obstetrical care where the rich and famous go for childbirths. This trend also has another advantage. Whereas previously healthcare professionals tend to work only in the public sector with a fixed salary, perhaps even with rigid career structure, the opening up of the private sector can offer them an alternative and flexible environment to work in. I have already seen many colleagues in China making this switch.

The privately led investment in healthcare in China can take many forms. It can be a privately funded hospital with modern facilities to provide comprehensive care for those with means or with private medical insurance. It can be a specialist hospital such as a cardiology centre, plastic/cosmetic centre, an obstetrical centre or an eye centre etc. There are also private run outpatient clinics, mainly as a group or syndicated practice. In addition, online personal telemedicine platforms for a fee are also available. This investment has been huge in the last 10 years. For instance, in 2016, the number of public hospitals of various grades in China was 12,708 while the number of private hospitals was 16,432. But in the year before, the number of private hospitals was 14,518, a staggering increase of nearly 13% within just a year. The total number of beds in public hospitals was 4,450,000. The total number of beds in private hospitals was 1,230,000 (while the figure for 2015 was 1,030,000, an increase in bed capacity of nearly 20% within a year). In other words, one in five hospital beds in China is in the private sector. This private/public sector split is most impressive. It is far above the level in the UK, which is an almost exclusively public-funded service while in the USA, it is an almost exclusively private-funded service, with the state chipping in as Medicare or Medicaid. This degree of public/private collaboration in China, in my opinion, can provide add-on value in enhancing and complementing each other's strength and thus offering huge potential and opportunities to ensure modern-day medical services can be effectively provided to all, based on both needs and the ability to pay.

An Emerging Public and Private Model

Such a public and private model of healthcare provision also has another attraction in terms of resource reallocation. The growth of the economy and its evolution from a manufacturing-based economy to a service-based economy has confirmed the marketability and profitability of such commercial healthcare insurance enterprises. The other main attraction is that since the state is the main stakeholder in providing basic healthcare, resources can be freed up to enable the state to focus on the promotion of primary care and public health to reach out to those vast regions which have not been developed as successful economically. There is still much important work in these areas that can only be done by the state. Such areas here include a nationwide coordinated planning in public health initiatives such as smoking cessation. China has a huge smoking population. The World Health Organization estimated that there are about 300 million smokers in China, about one third of the world's smokers. In addition, there are other equally important areas to tackle such as avoidance of alcoholism, lifestyle changes in the importance of a healthy diet and regular physical exercise, prevention, surveillance and control of any infectious outbreaks, early screening of diseases such as hepatitis, breast cancer, and bowel cancer.

One particular area of importance needing national attention which I would like to highlight is the problem of type 2 diabetes, which affects older people and is generally managed by medications and not insulin. I pointed this out because the incidence of type 2 diabetes in China is estimated to have reached 11% of the population currently whereas 30 years ago it was only 1%. One of the reasons is that as society becomes more modern and urban based, our diet becomes much more enriched with a high sugar content while we are doing much less physical exercise. There is also said to be a genetic disposition of Chinese to develop this disease. This form of diabetes is not difficult to diagnose, relatively cheap to treat but it does involve lifestyle adjustments. If early detection and treatment are initiated, it can delay or even prevent late complications such as cardiovascular, kidney, and eye problems, treatment of these late complications are expensive. Hospitals per se cannot solve these problems as diabetes patients often fail to attend follow-up to be monitored, but the state can by setting up national initiatives such as regular screening, public health education, and emphasising the need to attend clinics for assessment. Prevention of multiple complications is always better than treatment of complications. Having worked in China in the last few years, I have already noticed how information to the public at the outset of any epidemics, such as avian flu, was widely disseminated to the public through various media, how quickly the necessary, preventative, and control measures were put in place and how efficiently such outbreaks were contained. These noticeable improvements are not necessarily noticed, reported or appreciated in the West but credit where credit is due, China has already made significant strides in the public health arena. Smoking ban in public places is already successfully implemented in major cities and in HKU SZH, a smoking cessation clinic was set up about three years ago.

This model of private capital-driven investment in healthcare, however, is not without its own critics and can be under strain too. When it comes to insuring or investing in healthcare, major medical advances in new therapeutic and diagnosis are simply too rapid and the costs too high these days that even venture capitalists will think twice in trying to decide the worthiness of the investments in healthcare. In addition, medical investments are measured not in millions but in billions. The insurance companies will have to deal with this by clever marketing, by inserting more exclusion clauses (safety net being provided by the government), and by increasing the premium and asking themselves constantly, at what premium the customers will find affordable and acceptable to pay while the insurers can still make a profit. The phenomenal rise in costs is such that even the insurance companies have tended to list the latest advances, especially in cancer treatment and cellular therapies, into the exclusion lists for coverage. Yet the big pharmaceutical companies, which invested heavily into developing these advances, may also legitimately ask for investments returns, defined in their cases as profits. A case in point is the current debate on the healthcare system in the USA. The USA undoubtedly is the global leader in medical research and advances but the funding mechanism for new advances is a major area of huge domestic debate, even discord, from presidential elections to presidential elections. Yet, with all these years of debate, an agreed compromise is nowhere near to be reached. The perpetual question is: in any healthcare system, who should be the beneficiaries of the profits from a patented drug? Should it be the patients by reducing the price or the shareholders by paying a larger dividend? The free-market capitalist will say investors should be the beneficiaries while the socialists will say patients. The impartial idealists will say both.

The truth is, when it comes to healthcare funding, there is no perfect and universally acceptable model. This is a conundrum, no country has yet to come up with a model that will get the acceptance of both the users and the providers of medical service. China, because of its track records in modernisation, technology catch up, economic achievement, and its huge population of urban and suburban mix, may arguably have a real chance of coming up with a successful and acceptable model.

The Importance of Health Economics

There is, however, another way to look at the problem. Instead of looking purely on funding and the conflicts of ethics between the patient and the shareholder, one should, as a doctor or a healthcare manager, look at the practice of evidence-based, clinical and cost-effectiveness in the assessments of advances in therapeutics and diagnostics. This value-for-money approach is now known as health economics within the profession, with the UK taking a leading role in its earlier and pioneering work. This is certainly within our professional abilities and in doing so, protecting the interests of the patients. Organisations such as the Food and Drug Administration (FDA) in the USA and National Institute of Clinical Excellence (NICE) in the UK were set up for this purpose. The main difference is that FDA mainly deals in validating efficacy of treatments or diagnostics while NICE deals with cost-effectiveness as well. In China, the equivalent organisation is known as the China Food and Drug Administration (CFDA). All are government funded but independent organisations. The NICE team in the UK consists of a group of experienced health economists, managers, statisticians, people's representatives, well qualified doctors, and scientists, all actively engaging in carefully analysing the data and published information, often with additional raw data supplied by the pharmaceutical companies. My own personal experience when working as an advisor to NICE some years ago when I was in the UK was that it is very objective in assessing clinical effectiveness of a drug, or a test, to reach a recommendation to the government if it should be available and funded by the NHS. NICE is therefore an impartial mediator in assessing the health benefits of any new drug or tests.

Furthermore, one also needs to be aware that advances may turn out to be false dawns in the long term. Earlier claims are just earlier claims. It will take years to make a valid assessment. New drugs may ultimately not be translated into improved survival. The latest advances may be a trend but are not necessarily beneficial while old practices and treatments are not necessarily inferior. To seek long-term answers to these questions may take years, if not decades. Put it in another way, new drugs may not be as good as they are claimed while old drugs may not be as inferior as they are thought! Meanwhile, how do we decide? Resources are limited while new advances and information (often with slick and clever marketing by the pharmaceuticals) are made constantly, available directly to not only the professionals, but the public and patients as well. The drawback is that the public and the patient, because of their desperation to seek new treatment, may or may not be as discerning. Organisations such as CFDA, FDA, and NICE are set up to help to address these problems.

What can we, as medical practitioners, do to help? We cannot simply learn the new advances without knowing the cost implications. Cost containment and extra funding for advances are the twin brothers in medicine, one cannot proceed without the other, otherwise standards will deteriorate, or countries may be saddled with debt. The inflation of medical cost is always higher than the general inflation. Within the medical fraternity, there are now professional organisations, often nationally based, made up of senior and experienced specialists, in drawing up national recommendations or guidelines for standards of care or best practice. The aim is to set up a clinical model of pathways for all of us to follow. Expensive new drugs or genetic diagnostic tests may or may not be included in these guidelines. The advantages of these guidelines are that they are not rigid or prescriptive. New drugs are only recommended in these guidelines when they are thoroughly assessed by the clinical experts to be clinically effective. For example, in my own specialty, the treatment aim of a patient with acute leukaemia may be the same but the actual treatment (the various drugs and dosage to use) may vary.

In other words, there are standards and various treatment options to allow for some clinical flexibility. These guidelines not only are there to ensure uniformity of practice, but also limit the excessive use of unnecessary, expensive but unproven drugs or diagnostic tools based on trendiness and not on clinical benefits. In the past when I worked in the UK, I checked the UK guidelines on a regular basis and now in China, I check both the Chinese guidelines and the international ones, as a helpful external benchmark for my own practice.

CHAPTER 11

The First Three Years – from Nothing to Something

I arrived at HKU SZH on a steaming hot summer day on August 20th 2012. It was 7.45 a.m. I was met by a manager from the Human Resource Department. He gave me a brief introduction to the hospital. My first impression was that it was huge and spacious, but some key parts were yet to be finished. When I was first approached to take up the post a few months prior to this, I visited the site personally and it was then just a nearly completed hospital by looking at it from the outside. I was not allowed to go inside the building to have a look as parts of it were still under construction. After the introduction by the manager, I couldn't help thinking and wondering what a big challenge it was for me in taking up my post as the Chief of Service, covering nine medical subspecialties on a full-time contract of three years. These specialties are cardiology, respiratory medicine, gastroenterology/hepatology, neurology, dermatology, endocrinology, nephrology, rheumatology, and haematology (later on Intensive Care was added to this list). This is a huge hospital with six blocks, each block of seven floors high (housing a total bed capacity of 2,000) with a central nucleus block of five floors high housing all the outpatient areas, an Emergency Room underground, and all the diagnostics facilities, covering around 37,000 square metres in total. Clinical services initially were very limited. There were no inpatient beds then. Medicine had very rudimentary and skeleton outpatient services covering only very basic cardiology, respiratory, endocrinology, haematology, and nephrology. The number of Outpatient Department (OPD) attendance for Medicine in total was less than 50 per day. The only diagnostic tests we could request were blood counts, some basic biochemical tests, chest X-ray, and limited ultrasonography.

I was not disappointed, nor was I deterred, and I knew that much needed to be done. I was not daunted either, just utterly bemused by this amazing, huge environment. I told myself that not a single day was to be wasted. Though there were transport services provided for those of us who commuted from Hong Kong daily in a fleet of 7-seater cars, I chose not to use the service and instead decided to stay overnight from Mondays to Fridays, perhaps even Sundays, to reduce travel fatigue. A door-to-door return journey from my brother's home in Hong Kong, where I stayed, to the hospital takes four hours per day. This would mean I could gain an extra 20 hours of work time, instead of an energy sapping journey time, per week, by going back to Hong Kong only on Friday evenings.

The challenges for me were that not only did I have to familiarise myself with the new system in China, I also had to start recruiting and working with a new group of healthcare professionals from mainland China. This can be very difficult as our background and modus operandi were so different. I also needed to help the hospital to develop further key services, not only in Medicine, but also other major services such as Intensive Care Unit and a special Private Wing for the hospital. I had no time to waste. Very quickly and luckily, I got not only used to working with my mainland Chinese colleagues, I actually felt rejuvenated by the novelty of working with a whole new team. The challenge was real, but the mutual excitement and enthusiasm were the bond between us. I was made to feel very welcome by the warm hospitality of my mainland Chinese colleagues. All were hardworking, obliging, and ever so eager to find out how things were done in the UK, so my working with them was never boring.

The initial struggles and the unfamiliarity of the system which I found myself working in were gradually replaced by, with much personal satisfaction and relief, a feeling of heartfelt reward every time a new service was commissioned. To the present day, I can still remember very clearly in my mind the first ever haematology patient I saw in the outpatient, the first medical admission in October 2012, my first ward round, the first bone marrow biopsy, the first endoscopy, the first dialysis, the first ICU admission, the first cardiac catheterisation, the first bronchoscopy, and the first bone marrow transplant patient. These memories are still so vivid to me and so precious to behold.

Two things that HKU SZH pioneered right from the word Go was to set up an appointment system for outpatient consultation (walk-ins for those without an appointment of course were also allowed). Each outpatient appointment was allocated an average of 15 minutes to allow for a thorough consultation. Each doctor attending the Outpatient will have an average of 30-40 consultations per day, depending on the nature of the specialty. In China, often patients need to queue up first thing in the morning to get an appointment slot for the day. Appointment system for patients hardly existed. Worse still, in some big hospitals with a national reputation, there will be some 'agents' who would have, through some strange and inexplicable means, prearranged allocated slots to sell at a price. This was unique, opaque, and of course wrong. Or there may be people (not patients seeking medical attention) who are prepared to queue up to get a slot at the crack of dawn for a fee. At HKU SZH, an appointment system is the standard system. Initially, there were some teething problems, especially that patients found it difficult to adjust to this new appointment system. Over the ensuing few years, appointments not only became the norm but also widely adopted by other hospitals in China.

The other thing that HKU SZH did is to dispense with the presence of an intravenous (IV) infusion in a specially designated clinical area. In China, it is almost a standard practice that an IV infusion area is set up next to the Emergency Room (ER) while the real clinical necessity for this IV infusion is not too apparent. Overuse of IV infusion has always been an observation uniquely prevalent in China. So, even though such an area was planned in the original architectural design, one of the earliest bold decisions that the senior management of HKU SZH made was to do away with this area. Space is always at a premium in any hospital and such a clinical area could be much better utilised for other key services. In our case, this area was converted into a peaceful and calming clinic area for Traditional Chinese Medicine (TCM). It later turned out that the doing away of an IV infusion area was in fact never a subject of complaints either by the public or the healthcare officials in Shenzhen. It was not only the right decision, but an easy one too.

Progress After First Three Years

With the collective will of the hospital management, government support, and the dedication of staff, we were gradually able to develop into a truly comprehensive acute hospital with a 2,000-bed capacity. OPD attendance has increased steadily to an average currently of more than 6,000 per day and 3,000 on Saturdays with a waiting time of no more than two working days for any patients needing a specialty consultation. All General Practice and Specialty clinics are now available daily Mondays to Saturdays. There are a total of at least 11 sessions per specialty per week and for some specialties with high demands such as cardiology, respiratory medicine, Saturday afternoon session is also available, making it a total of 12 sessions per week. This is unheard of in the UK where waiting time for specialty consultation appointments is measured in weeks, if not months, rather than in less than two days. This long waiting time for a specialist opinion in the UK was such a problem that a specific performance target was set up by the government to shorten the specialty appointment waiting time and still, the waiting time currently is weeks for most specialties. There is virtually no such waiting time in China. I am very impressed and proud of this as it is clearly in the interests of the patients. The other very notable effect, which is also important to point out, is that this will undoubtedly offload the pressure that Emergency Room (ER) faces, with the result that emergency conditions will be dealt with speedily and effectively by ER team, so waiting time in ER is hardly ever a problem, unlike in the UK when every winter there will be crisis in the ER. At HKU SZH, if ER wishes to seek a specialty opinion for a certain patient, it can initiate a specialist referral to have the specialist come down to ER or refer the patient to the appropriate clinic on the same day, without any need for another trip to the hospital by the patient.

To support all these services, nearly all the diagnostic and support services are now available in the same clinical and central block which houses the laboratories, the radiological and ultrasound services, endoscopy and dialysis services, with a robotic transport system called the rails (built onto the ceilings like little movable trolleys) for transporting the blood samples and drugs deliveries. CT requests are handled within a few days of requests while MR may take a week, but in an emergency, even MR can be done within a day, with staff almost always working overtime willingly to finish the work. Apart from some complex molecular or genetic tests, which are outsourced, most laboratory-based diagnostic tests are done in-house. All requests are generated electronically, and all samples contain a 2D barcode, which cuts down much labelling time both in the clinical front end and at the processing area in the laboratories. I once had a blood test for a routine check in late afternoon and by the next morning, I could check the results on my smartphone.

Though HKU SZH now boasts a figure of 6,000 outpatient attendances during the week, it does also give out the impression that it is run very efficiently. Gone are the days when I witnessed in the UK where Outpatient Services were overrun by clerks rushing around with trolleys to get the notes ready for clinics, and clinics reception areas full of case notes or porters running around with blood samples. In HKU SZH, I walk past the outpatient clinics twice a day, I do not see any trolleys or staff rushing around, and certainly not bulky paper case notes in clinics. Just like a well-run international airport, the OPD gives out an impression that it is busy and efficiently run, there is no sense of disorderliness.

As mentioned before, every morning at around 7.00 a.m., there is a fleet of 12 passenger cars of six- or seven-seaters departing from Hong Kong, from three collecting points in Hong Kong Island and Kowloon for the HKU staff who need to come to HKU SZH, arriving about 8.30 a.m. This is usually a combination of senior managers, doctors, and professors who together form a core senior management team for the hospital. This management team works closely with our mainland Chinese colleagues so the expertise at

Queen Mary's Hospital (QMH), where the HKU clinical academic staff work, can be developed with and supported by our mainland colleagues.

The Strife for National and International Quality

In China, the hallmark of a hospital's achievement in terms of services and quality is a grading system, not dissimilar to the UK system of Care Quality Commission (CQC), where all aspects of the day-to-day management, safety, and services are studied and scrutinised in detail every few years. The top grade in China is listed as 3A and only the very best hospitals can be awarded a 3A rating. There are very strict inspection rules and tight marking systems. The requirements, especially detailed documentation, are both exacting and exhausting. This may range from the management of different waste disposal systems, to the detailed knowledge of incident management, fire drills, to the front-line use of blood products, consents, and clinical records etc. I feel that by going through this very thorough inspection, I know far more about the hospital than I had previously. At HKU SZH, this inspection was carried by a national team of approved experts for a whole week in 2017, and much to the credit and hard work of all the staff, HKU SZH was awarded a 3A rating. In the whole of China, there were a total of 1,308 3A accredited hospitals in 2016. Even before we were ready for this 3A application and for a few years prior to that, HKU SZH also applied to another quality accreditation system recognised internationally as ACHS (the Australian Council on Healthcare Standards). HKU SZH achieved full accreditation from ACHS in 2016. The reason why ACHS was also chosen was because this was the accreditation system used by government-funded public hospitals in Hong Kong, including QMH. So, by the end of 2017,

HKU SZH was the only hospital in China achieving the remarkable feat of receiving such dual accreditation, one national, and the other international. Such recognition was the result of collective will power, determination, and selfless dedication by all the staff. One only has to imagine the scale of the tasks in translating the documents from Chinese to English and vice versa during the years of preparation for the ACHS and 3A accreditation to appreciate the scale of the tasks involved.

Efficiency and Productivity

One of the other distinctive aspects of the China health services is its emphasis on efficiency and productivity, especially on the number of patients seen in the OPD and the turnaround time of the diagnostic tests. There are good and laudable reasons for this. The public hospitals have to balance their annual income with their annual expenditure and bonus paid to the staff is often dependent on this balance. So there is a constant need to drive up innovation, efficiency, and productivity, using a business model of 'the more you serve or sell, the more income you will generate' and thus the more you have to invest or reward staff (the customer is king concept in running a public-funded hospital). I have been both an inpatient and outpatient in HKU SZH and so will quote a few personal experiences to illustrate this point.

A few months ago, I had a cold sore and needed some topical cream. It took me, from the time the prescription was given to me by the dermatologist, to the time it took to get this cream into my hand, a total of 20 minutes. This included paying at the cashier for the item (could have been even faster if I could use one of the Alipay machines in the outpatient area, instead of paying cash) and then going to and waiting at the OPD pharmacy, where it has a modern German-made robotic dispenser. The most remarkable thing is that by the time I reached the Pharmacy waiting area, the huge screen display was already displaying the information indicating my name and which counter to go to for the item, similar to which boarding gate to go to for a departing flight. This efficiency of such a short waiting time for a prescribed medication is something that the UK NHS could not have matched.

At HKU SZH, patients can also book or change an OPD appointment on our website or log on to find our hospital on an app called WeChat, which is now nationally seen as the app of all apps in China. Patients can also choose to arrange an appointment by phone, or even choose to arrive in person on the same day. Just as going to see a film in the cinema, there are a multitude of ways to get a medical appointment at the time of the patient's choice. The waiting time is usually no more than two days and often can be the same day of the request. This is something which is unheard of in many other advanced healthcare systems. The doctors arrive no later than 8.30 a.m. in the clinics every morning or 2 p.m. in the afternoon. Late arrivals of the doctors at the clinics will be recorded and assessed as an ongoing performance indicator for each department, among many other indicators. The waiting time for the actual consultation is no more than an hour, with an appointment on an individual display screen in each clinic, together with a TV explaining the workings of the hospital set-up with patient information for various diseases. For instance, in the diabetic clinics, there will be education pamphlets and video information on diabetes. In the OPD, one of the major reforms introduced at HKU SZH for any doctor attending the clinics is to see an average of 30-40 patients per day, depending on the specialty. The aim is not only to avoid overworking the doctors but also to avoid doctors seeing too many patients. In nearly all public hospitals in China, the pay or the bonus for the doctors is often linked to the number of patients seen. This has led some doctors to seeing more than 80 patients a day, with some barely given a few minutes of consultation.

Another reform in HKU SZH is that the patients cannot choose a particular named doctor to see, while in other hospitals this is acceptable. The principle here is the service is specialty-based, team-based and not individual-based, similar to the system in the UK. For those patients who particularly wish to see a consultant from Hong Kong or mainland China, they can choose to go to the private wing of HKU SZH called the International Medical Centre (IMC), which will be briefly described later.

The main difference between HKU SZH and others in China is that there is also, for six days a week, a General Practitioners (GP) Outpatient Service, much like the UK system except that this GP service is based on-site within the main block of the hospital. Patients with non-specific symptoms or ailments can choose to attend such a service. In addition, the GP Outpatient Service is backed by all the specialties. So if for example a situation arises that a GP needs to refer someone with a very high white cell count, suggesting a possible leukaemic process, then there is no need for another referral, the patient needs only be advised to go upstairs to book a same day appointment to see a haematologist.

If a patient is to be admitted, then there is always a bed at HKU SZH for the patient. There are currently no such phenomena as shortage of beds, much less the terrible phenomenon of temporary camp beds. In a situation where there is a shortage of beds in a given specialty, there is a well-organised triage system of admitting the patients directly to another ward, closely coordinated by the ward nurses, on a day-to-day basis if need be. This is a very important point to highlight as, in many other hospitals in China, some ill patients needing hospital admission can often be told that there is no bed and asked to seek attention elsewhere. In short, if a haematology patient needs admission while there is no haematology bed, then the doctor is likely to advise the patient to seek services and beds at another hospital, which can be nearby or some distance away. At HKU SZH, turning away patients from any specialty is not a hospital policy, and every effort is made to attend to the needs of every patient.

Other Areas of Good Practice

In addition, there are other practices which in my view are truly aligned with international good practices, not even seen in many UK public hospitals, even for those hospitals which enjoy international recognition for their expertise and competence. Good practices in China need special mention and should be shared and learned from. I shall try to discuss them one by one in some detail.

In China, the 3A standards state that there should always be a doctor in the ward 24/7, for an average ward of between 36-44 beds. At HKU SZH, the average ward capacity is 40-44. During the official lunch break between 12.00 p.m. and 1.30 p.m., there must also be a doctor in the ward on a rota basis. He or she will not be allowed to go to any educational or other meetings during the lunch break. Lunch will be brought to the doctors' office. Equally and more impressively, each ward will have a resident in the evening and all through the weekend. Each ward will also have its own on-call room with a small pantry and a shower room for the residents. Seeing ill patients or admitting new patients will therefore have no delays. Nurses in the ward need hardly ever page the on-call doctors and in fact, pagers are no longer used in China, but rather smartphones. This will improve patient care as clinical problems are dealt with without any delays and nurses are much more reassured. In addition, there is no need for cross cover for other specialties for the first-tier resident on call. In other words, each specialty provides its first-tier on-call cover by its own pool of residents, backed up by a second tier of senior doctors. This will enhance continuation of care and make the daily handovers much more efficient.

Because of the above, the handover the next morning is not only structured, but well documented in a handover book so the incoming team would know of any change in clinical conditions of the patients from the night before. The handover takes place at 8.15 a.m. every morning during the week. On weekends, the residents for the previous night do not normally leave until about 11.00 a.m. after the proper handover to the duty doctor who arrives at 8.30 a.m. is completed. The nurses have a similar structured handover process too. I have often been very impressed by this, as good continued care must be accompanied by a good handover system, something which I struggled to see in the UK. The handover system in the UK, though emphasised, is not structured except perhaps in the Intensive Care Unit or Operating Theatres.

One other area of good practice is the quality of the case notes documentation through the use of an integrated hospital clinical IT system. In some advanced hospitals in the UK, case notes are no longer necessary, but the information contained in the system may not be comprehensive. In China, the inpatient case notes requirements are very strict and of very high standards. The standards of these notes, especially their contents, the level of their details, and the completeness of the information required are very much part of an ongoing and monthly performance indicator for each department. Every part of the case notes will be checked, including laboratory results, pathology or X-ray reports, consent forms for surgeries, procedures, and blood transfusions. In addition, the clinical day-to-day entries in the notes have to be signed for. So, for instance, when I do a professorial ward round twice a week, I have to sign for my entries for that round. There will be, on the front page of the record, an admission summary and on discharge, a full discharge summary will be handed to the patient who can then go home with detailed information, with all the relevant diagnosis based on ICD codes, including the medications list. The quality and timeliness of the completed case returns are then assessed before taken for central filing; the assessment results will be sent to the Chief of Services monthly as a performance indicator. The standard time limit for a completed filing of medical records is set at seven working days. In addition, there is also random, snapshot audit in the ward by nurses from other wards to cross-check each other on the case notes quality.

It was on October 24th 2012 when the first Medical inpatient was admitted. At the time, I personally found that the demands on the quality of the case notes were a bit too strict, tiresome even. At the beginning, we in the Department of Medicine never reached a 90% filing rate (the standard for a complete record to be filed is within seven working days). Not only was our filing rate poor but the content rating was also poor, graded at either B or C (the standard required is at least 95% or above should be A).

Now, eight years later, the medical records filing rate from every specialty of the hospital is nearly 100% (with the occasional 98%!) for its timeliness and more than 95% for its contents (Grade A), both in compliance with national requirements. As far as I am aware, neither

Hong Kong nor the UK has such standards. I am now fully converted and committed to such a performance indicator for detailed and timely documentation. Such detailed case notes can be a powerful piece of evidence and an effective means of verification in times of dispute or complaints, an area which I shall touch on later. It would not be far off when one day the paper case notes documentation can be replaced by electronic case notes, as some hospitals both in the UK and China are doing. Imagine the savings on paper and its effect on the environment if a country with 1.4 billion people all trying to reduce paper consumption in a complicated area like the medical services!

If a patient on discharge needs to be seen by another specialty, such as if one of my patients with diabetes who has been put on corticosteroid for a haematological condition needs to have his/her blood sugar assessed in the endocrinology clinic, I do not need to start another referral letter as the discharge letter will have stated that an endocrinology consultation is needed. Not only does it avoid duplication, but also gives the patient a choice of which hospital to seek such attention from. The detailed discharge summary will serve as a self-explanatory referral. In modern days, it is emphasised that the referral letter should be factual and impartial without any use of subjective, descriptive words which may upset the patients. A discharge letter given to the patient can overcome this problem.

Outpatient or inpatient cross-specialty referrals are very much part of a day-to-day necessity in any major hospital and our hospital is no exception. Specialties like cardiology, respiratory, general surgery, orthopaedics, endocrinology receive numerous daily referrals for inpatients. The benchmark for these cross-specialty referrals is so efficiently set that all non-urgent referrals must be seen within 24 hours of the referrals while urgent ones must be dealt with within 30 minutes from the time when the request for consultation is made, and often such urgent referrals are accompanied by a phone call. These referrals are all electronically made and alerted, much like an alert on a smart mobile device, so time can be recorded and tracked, making sure that cross-referral consultations are dealt with in a timely manner.

If a senior input for a complicated case is needed, such as advice from consultants, it will be organised on a multidisciplinary team (MDT) basis, attendance and discussions are all documented. Those specialties invited must send a senior representative and the referral of such a complicated case will be emailed via the internal system to the receiving specialties. So, for example, if I have to attend such a meeting where haematology input is needed, I would have been sent a full clinical information sheet on the email rather than getting there and then learning of the problem. This is especially important when a radiologist's opinion is needed. In other hospitals in China, such MDT is organised by the Clinical Affairs Department but in our hospital, this is done by the internal email system. To protect patient confidentiality, the hospital clinical IT system is a stand-alone system which is entirely separated from the external system connected to the internet. Each user of the hospital IT system will be issued with a pen drive and a self-created passcode. When I attend such an MDT, requested by another specialty, say for a complicated blood clotting problem, the discussion around the table will consist of several relevant specialties but the key information such as radiological images, biopsy report, or results of blood tests will always be displayed on a projection screen from the hospital IT system.

In China, there are other good standards which are worth mentioning, and which HKU SZH is fully compliant with. These include not only the widespread and regular use of MDT, but also that any patient with an uncertain diagnosis within three working days from admission would also need to be discussed. Furthermore, if clinical progress is such that the patient's condition becomes more complicated, then there must be a recorded discussion of these complex cases, outside the consultant ward round. In other words, complex cases or those with uncertain diagnosis would receive special attention and effort.

For patients who pass away during their stay in the hospital, then there must be a documented mortality meeting within seven working days when the case would be thoroughly reviewed by the medical staff of the specialty responsible, to see if any improvement can be made or lessons learned. This mortality meeting is a national standard in China with which HKU SZH is also fully compliant. This is also desired in the UK but in fact, hardly ever properly implemented.

Antibiotic stewardship is widely practised, and its importance respected. Infection Control is one of the Areas of Excellence (AOEs) at HKU SZH. Its importance is appreciated by all at HKU SZH. To prevent the emergence and the control of antibiotic resistant strain of bacteria, there is now a national standard of antibiotic usage that all hospitals need to be compliant with. Use and misuse of antibiotics are closely monitored. Issues such as multi-resistant organisms, catheter-associated infections are all promptly managed, data recorded and regularly discussed, using national benchmarks as a guide for hospital or departmental performance. The antibiotic usage is also mandatory agenda items discussed monthly at both the management and departmental levels. For instance, since I am in charge of the haemato-oncology and haematopoietic stem cell transplant services, I will have data available to me on our defined daily dose (DDD) to assess the appropriateness of our use and our choice of any oral or intravenous antibiotics and the duration of our use.

Expertise in Keyboard Skills

One of the most amazing things I noticed shortly after my arrival is to see the way my colleagues type Chinese and their use of the keyboard. I was never trained to type and for years, I did not need to type as most of the times I either wrote in the notes or used a Dictaphone for any work that needed typing, which then would be done by the clerical staff. It was only in my forties that I started to type when the internet and the email came along. So I learned to type due to needs and not due to interest. Over the years, one tends to take it for granted that the standard keyboard with all the symbols and the English letters is the global standard. I often wondered in the past that for the Chinese language, will there ever be a Chinese typing machine? I was taught that to be proficient in the use of the Chinese language, one needs to know about 3,000 essential and individual characters, totally unlike the English language where every word is made up of essentially the same 26 letters. Not only does one need to know the 3,000 basic characters in Chinese, one also has to remember each individual pronunciation, while most English words can be worked out or guessed at by the combination of the letters. Every keyboard I see in China and in my Shenzhen hospital is exactly the same as the English standard keyboard, and yet the typing speed of our Chinese colleagues is just as fast as in the West. I was so impressed by their ability in using a standard keyboard to type Chinese. There is no need to develop another keyboard specifically for the Chinese language.

The reason for the above is simple yet ingenious. It turned out that all Chinese people are educated to learn the phonetics for the pronunciation of Chinese characters in *pinyin* (which is the standardised phonetic system for *putonghua*) based on the English letters. So, when they use the standard keyboard to type Chinese words, all they need to do is key in the English letters according to *pinyin*, with the software designed to automatically translate the input into the corresponding Chinese words. For example, if I wish to type the message 'how are you' in Chinese, I would type 'ni hao ma', which is the way 'how are you' is spoken in *putonghua*, and the Chinese words will be displayed. Since the *pinyin* system uses the English letters, the users are familiar with the standard keyboard. This conversion to keyboard and the convenience are further enhanced by predictive texts and words. The software is so clever these days that often in medicine, once a combination of words is frequently used, the next word will be automatically displayed, such as if you type the word 'head', the word 'headache' will also be displayed as an option. So nearly everything I read at HKU SZH is always typed neatly in Chinese in electronic form, and this also makes filing of documentation easier, unless of course, it is a Post-it note (which serves an entirely different function), consisting of only a few words. Years ago, when I was in the UK, I had daily on my desks averaging 30 letters, notes, information leaflets of all sorts, but now in China, I hardly receive any paper letters or notices on my desk. Nearly all forms are electronic and paperless. This is by far more convenient and efficient. In the past, I used to get phone calls regularly when the caller checked if I received a certain letter, which, after much checking, only to tell the caller that I had not received that letter. In China and in this paperless world, this has changed, and tracking is far easier and robust.

Technology will continue to improve. We are now seeing a handwriting pad and even speech recognition software. I personally still prefer keyboard typing and would not like to see the day when no one types and everyone just talks to a gadget. The art of handwriting is already dwindling but hopefully not typing, as typing still involves tactile skill of our fingers, and is the nearest thing to writing.

Nursing Developments and Performance Indicators

In the first few years after I started the inpatient haematology services, the nursing standard, though good in general, did experience some difficulties because of the complexities involved in nursing care in this specialty involving aggressive chemotherapies, use of various blood products and antibiotics, management of indwelling intravenous devices and above all, dealing with anxious patients and families. The turnover rate of nurses in our department was high. However, the situation has now improved greatly as the initial inexperienced nurses have now become experienced. The hospital also holds regular nurse training sessions to which attendance is high with attendance records electronically kept. One classic recent example is how well our nurses are prepared and trained in dealing with the COVID-19 outbreak and how familiar they are with the use of the protective gowns. I feel so very reassured and enlightened now. There is a difference in nursing practice in China compared with the West. The nurses in China mainly implement medical decisions but their extended clinical roles are relatively limited. I very much hope that this can be improved as the nursing profession is the largest group of front-line staff in any hospital. Their contribution will be crucial. Just like the practice in the West, senior nurses can be trained and empowered to carry out other invasive procedures like endoscopies, bone marrow biopsies, liver biopsies, neckline insertions, even writing some predetermined prescriptions, which are common in the West. The development of these extended clinical roles can only benefit the patients as the care can be more speedily provided. For instance, in our own bone marrow transplant (BMT) centre, we now have a BMT coordinator who is a nurse by background. She plays an important role in our service, acting like a counsellor, a doctor, a nurse, a trainer, and a main hands-on operator for our blood cells separator (more on this in Chapter 27).

For those of us who have a senior managerial role in a department, we are regularly supplied with, on a monthly basis, a whole variety of key and useful information. This will include our monthly workload figures, our adverse incidents relating to drugs, patients' complaints or compliments, with complaints required to be dealt with and an explanation provided within a week. Untoward incidents will be reported and analysed to form part of an ongoing CQI (continued quality improvement programme) for each department. Patients' experience surveys are carried out on a regular basis by departments, in an effort to improve the overall quality of patients' experiences in the hospital.

Patients also have access, either online or on paper, to their diagnostic information and results of any tests from a special hospital website using specific patient identification numbers to protect privacy. Diagnostic information or results of tests are instantly available to the patients. I found it a truly rewarding experience when during a ward round, patients on chemotherapy for remission induction for acute leukaemia could actually tell me, by the bedside, what his/her latest neutrophil count was that very day and what his renal function test was the previous day. I do my ward round at 9.30 a.m., the blood tests are usually done before 7.00 a.m. and the results are usually available on the screen then. The team will spend around 8.30 a.m. to 9.30 a.m. to get up to speed with all the latest diagnostic information. The turnaround time for these diagnostic tests is usually very quick. I once had a young but ill patient admitted to the ward directly from our afternoon clinic around 5.00 p.m. which was the time she arrived at the ward. She was then seen by our resident, and by 7.00 p.m. I had all the results of laboratory tests needed for me to take the necessary clinical measures.

Most inpatients do not have a laptop with them but all of them have a smartphone which connects them with the outside world, be it their families, TV entertainment, or even the results of their own diagnostic tests, which they often show me in the ward round. In China, they are not only our patients, young or old, but they are also modern-day netizens. With the soon-to-be available 5G smartphone, it is entirely possible to visualise a future when consultations can be effectively conducted not only for inpatients but outpatients too, even patients from far away. This is known as telemedicine and is already being practised in some countries, including China. This telemedicine service will undoubtedly become more sophisticated, more effective, conducted over the internet by streaming. This is a service model which some hospitals are already actively exploring, thus launching and unleashing the full potential which the age of streaming can provide us with additional tools to improve the versatility and flexibility of medical services.

Countries like China or the US are ideal for such a major change due to the huge geographical landmass and differences in population density from urban cities to far out villages or towns. Indeed, I was impressed when once I visited a very remote village where the main activity was farming, houses were made of concrete and were very small. There I saw residents not actually watching TV as they might have done only five to 10 years ago but now they were nearly always sitting outside, in the open air, looking at their smartphone, chatting with friends, watching the news, or networking using WeChat. Such technology can equally be very speedily applied to other aspects of health care, especially in the primary care sectors, in public health issues such as a flu epidemic. Medical consultation over 5G will not be far away from now. Not to use it to improve healthcare will be a big opportunity missed and wasted.

Maternity leave is respected and admirably managed. The implementation of the maternity leave standards is based on national and local hospital Human Resources Department policies. With the abolishment of the One Child Policy, need for maternity leave is a day-to-day management reality and necessity, often a challenge as well. For a big department like the Department of Medicine at HKU SZH, which has nine sub-specialties, this can be problematic as nearly two thirds of our medical staff and more than 90% of nurses are females. In the UK, the gaps in staffing are often managed by having temporary staff. For medical doctors, these are called locums and for nurses, these are called bank nurses. But in the UK, even the most responsive recruitment process cannot ensure the qualities of the locums or the bank nurses. There would be gaps. In China and HKU SZH, there is no such option of temporary appointment. On a personal basis, I do not support the concept of temporary staff as it takes time to train them up to standard and for them to get familiar with the way the system works in any given hospital. It will be a risk management and safety issue for us. At HKU SZH, our medical staff view this in a very collegiate and sensible way. They just get on with it and share out the extra workload, including on call. It can of course be difficult at times, but the collective spirits are such that all of us will help each other by running an extra mile. It does not mean that their dedication is taken for granted and where necessary, the appropriate remuneration for extra duties will be awarded. They all take it in good faith. In the next chapter, I will describe in some detail how a specific 24/7 clinical service in the Department of Medicine was set up, as an illustration of my experience in China.

CHAPTER 12

Commissioning of the First 24/7 Interventional Services for Ischaemic Stroke in the Department of Neurology, HKU SZH

This section was written as an example to show the efforts and processes of how the first life-saving interventional 24/7 service at HKU SZH was commissioned in the Department of Medicine, for which I was at the time the full-time Chief of Service (COS) from August 2012 to July 2015. Since then, I have changed to a part-time contract and continued to head the Department of Haematology as a subspecialty within the Department of Medicine.

Stroke is a medical emergency. It means that something suddenly is happening in the circulation of the blood vessels in the brain, often manifesting itself as a sudden loss of consciousness or paralysis. It can be due to a blocked blood vessel and the resulting ischaemic (lack of blood supply) damage to the cells in the affected part of the brain, just like a heart attack. It can also be due to a burst blood vessel, leading to bleeding into the brain. Of the two, ischaemic strokes are more common and much more treatable. Both forms of strokes are serious conditions that can be fatal.

In England, one in six people will have a stroke in their lifetime, and new statistics released by Public Health England (PHE) show that 57,000 people had their first-time stroke in 2016. It is estimated that around 30% of people who have a stroke will go on to experience another stroke. Stroke is a leading cause of death and disability in the UK. There are around 32,000 stroke-related deaths in England each year. However, deaths related to stroke have declined by 49% in the past 15 years. This has been credited to a combination of better prevention, rapid diagnosis, and earlier treatment of ischaemic stroke. Getting an NHS health check for risk factors, such as smoking, hypertension, or diabetes, for those aged 40 to 74 years, can help to identify early if one is at risk of a stroke.

While the majority (59%) of strokes occurs in the older generation, PHE figures also found that over a third (38%) of first-time strokes happen in middle-aged adults (between the age of 40 and 69). More first-time strokes are now occurring at an earlier age compared to a decade ago. There are three types of strokes: ischaemic strokes from a clot, haemorrhagic stroke from bleeding, and a transient ischaemic stroke from a tiny clot from which symptoms resolved in 24 hours. Of all the three types of stroke, ischaemic stroke accounts for about 80% and is most amenable for timely treatment. Furthermore, the average age for males having a stroke fell from 71 to 68 years and for females, 75 to 73 years between 2007 and 2016. This data, demonstrating the increased incidence of strokes especially in the younger population, was from England. As I do not have similar data for China, there is no reason to suggest to me that this trend cannot be extrapolated to China. And since Shenzhen is a city with an expanding population with a younger age profile, all the more reasons for HKU SZH to set up an integrated clinical service for strokes.

Treatment of ischaemic stroke is available by the infusion of the drug tPA (tissue plasminogen activator) which can minimise damage by dissolving the clot. This is known as thrombolytic therapy, also known commonly as clot busting therapy. The guidelines published in 2018 by the American Heart Association and the American Stroke Association stated that tPA is more effective when it is given within four and a half hours from the start of a stroke which is the time of the onset of the first symptoms. One of the most widely used markers for this is the Door to Needle (DTN) time, which starts from the time when the patient arrives at the Emergency Room to the infusion of tPA. In fact, the sooner the better the outcome will be. Yet the infusion of tPA is not without its side effect, mainly bleeding, so speed and caution are both needed. In addition to this medical therapy, there is also the surgical therapy via a surgical interventional procedure involving removing the clot with a retrievable stent. This procedure is called embolectomy. So in order to achieve the most effective benefits of treatment, there are two essential components. The speed of the patient in reaching the Emergency Room and the speed of our thrombolysis team to assess and start the treatment.

Not only the speed of treatment is of essence here, it would also have to be a 24/7 service, an all-or-none service, part-time service is simply unacceptable. The symptoms have to be recognised quickly, especially by the staff in the Emergency Room, supported by speedy and detailed neurological assessment by our neurologists, backed up by neurosurgeons, diagnostic services such as CT scan, laboratories, and pharmacists, followed later on by rehabilitation services with physiotherapists. So this is a 24/7 service working as a truly multidisciplinary basis involving various specialties.

My neurologist colleagues and I started to plan for this from early 2013 by getting the various stakeholders involved, looking at the national standards and the data, modelling our aspirations to reach international standards. We held extensive training sessions for staff involved and started a detailed clinical pathway for the stroke patients. Risk assessments were carried out to test our state of readiness as infusion of tPA is not without risk, and so a check list has to be made before infusion, and the speed of therapy is of real essence here.

Our Achievements

This service started 12 months later, in March 2014. For the first time, I shall proceed to release here and present publicly our key results using our own in-house comprehensive database. From March 2014 to May 2019, there were 132 patients with ischaemic strokes treated by the Neurology Department at HKU SZH. It was worth noting that out of those 132 patients, 106 of them were treated between January 2016 and May 2019. This significant increase in activity in the last three years was because the team also launched a public education programme in the media and gave public lectures in the civil hall where the need for the patients to recognise early symptoms and attend ER is emphasised. Of these 132 patients who received tPA infusion, 21 of them had an embolectomy as well. The median DTN time of this cohort was 66.5 minutes. The median DTN time at first for 2014 was 115 minutes, while the median DTN time for 2018 was reduced markedly to 50 minutes. The rate of symptomatic intra cerebral haemorrhage (sICH) from the infusion of thrombolytic therapy was 6% (8/132). These results of our figures are entirely consistent with the global standards and performance targets.

So, over the last few years, a comprehensive stroke service has now been fully established and the unit has now been designated as one of the approved stroke centres, not only in the city of Shenzhen, but a national centre as well. Other specialised services, such as 24/7 PCI (primary cardiac intervention for coronary heart disease or suspected heart attacks) and endoscopic services for acute gastrointestinal bleeding have also been established at HKU SZH based on a similar approach of benchmarking with international and national standards.

CHAPTER 13

My Observations

The name of this chapter does imply that I can only see things from my own perspective. No healthcare system in the world is perfect. All hospitals are the same and yet all hospitals are different. Aiming to achieve a perfect healthcare system is unrealistic and unachievable. Getting better is the more realistic and acceptable aim. High standards are achievable, but the best standards are not. The word best is very hard to define here. The more realistic and appropriate way of looking at this is to make sure high standards are the norms for all. All systems have flaws, from the debates on the funding mechanism to the consideration of cultural diversification, the needs and expectations of the people in the delivery of healthcare, and variations in the epidemiological patterns of diseases. In life, all of us want different things with different expectations, varying from different tastes in clothes, in food, in interests. Above all, the common mindset is that we all want the best at the cheapest or, if not, the most affordable price. We tend to know in general the cost of something, be it a blood test or a new car, and if we do not know, we can always check the cost on the information superhighway. Yet often we are not sure about the true value of that something. Knowing the cost of something is different from knowing the value of something.

This is no more noticeable than in the delivery of healthcare to different groups with different diseases, some have common diseases, others have not so common diseases, or common diseases with a rare underlying cause, such as the diagnosis of a small but non-life threatening tumour in an adrenal gland above the kidney in a young patient with hypertension. The diagnosis of such a tumour as the cause for the hypertension requires significant clinical expertise, and sophisticated tests for confirmation. Some diseases may need a highly specialised team of skilled personnel, such as heart lung transplant for severe pulmonary hypertension and heart failure, when other medical therapies fail. For cases such as these, it can be difficult especially in a healthcare system like that in China. The value of the treatment simply cannot be quantified by adding up the charges mathematically of all the items of services such as blood tests, imaging, procedure costs or surgical costs, outpatient visits, number of hospital inpatient stay, theatre times. The whole process of the discussion, planning and execution would be impossible to work out meaningfully in an itemised fashion in complicated cases like these. In other words, what is chargeable and what is not chargeable? How would the real expertise and benefits be calibrated? The provision of such a complicated service, requiring a highly trained and dedicated specialised team of personnel, is only provided in the UK in a few selected cities spread out geographically. This is known as quaternary services, which are available only in a few approved centres in the UK. The aim here is to pool all the limited skills and resources together to ensure better outcomes and cost-effectiveness. So, any healthcare system will have to consider the needs of the people, the epidemiological data, and the individual, and strike a right balance for the reasons discussed above.

China is probably facing a much bigger challenge than others here. Quite apart from the debates on the funding mechanism (pricing and charging will be discussed later in Chapter 16), there is also the consideration for dealing with the cultural attitudes of the patients and their families. With the improvement of living standards and the emerging middle class, the patients' expectations are naturally higher than in the past. These high expectations can be heavily influenced by their cultural attitude and can be different even within close members of the family. It is not uncommon for me to experience that on diagnosing a patient with acute leukaemia, the parents of the patient, out of pure anxiety, concern, and overprotection for the patient, urge me to proceed with chemotherapy without telling the patient the diagnosis, its treatment, and prognosis. They may even tell me that they will sign the consent form for treatment. This to me is clearly unacceptable. In China, just like anywhere, the need for an informed consent for treatment is paramount and mandatory.

The other phenomenon in China, apart from shielding the patient from the diagnosis, is that on hearing the diagnosis, families may well be advised by their friends or other family members to seek treatment in another hospital. This of course I can accept, patients must be allowed and respected in making their choice. When I first started at HKU SZH, I did have patients whose families wished to seek attention elsewhere once the diagnosis of leukaemia was made. I was initially quite taken aback by this and even wondered why. I myself was used to the practice in the UK, where on breaking such bad news, we would sit down with the patients and their families, with a counsellor where possible, to reassure, to explain the ins and outs of the treatment, while also offer an element of hope and in so doing, obtain their informed consent for treatment. In China, the tendency to go elsewhere for diagnosis and treatment not only is prevalent, it also possibly reflects an element of disbelief or even lack of trust in the local hospital or doctor. So quite often when cancer or leukaemia is diagnosed, the patients and their families might choose to be discharged and then go to another big and famous 3A hospital for treatment. In the UK, a patient diagnosed with leukaemia is unlikely to be asking for transfer to London or other major cities for treatment.

However, in the last few years, there has been a marked improvement in this, much to the credit of our hardworking and dedicated team. This improvement is directly the result of the HKU SZH policy of emphasising communication with and open disclosure to patients and families. This has gained widespread confidence and trust by the community. I hope that with the progressive rise in living standards, improvement in education and the emergence of a better-informed middle class, trust between patients and doctors can improve more. In fact, I am sure it will, based on what has been observed at HKU SZH. This improvement will be nationwide.

CHAPTER 14

The Role of Traditional Chinese Medicine

The other cultural practice which must be accepted is on the practice of traditional Chinese medicine (TCM). TCM is very much an integral part of the long civilisation in China, used and well accepted by the people throughout the five thousand years of Chinese history. Documented work resembling textbooks and description of the practice of TCM started to appear originally during the time of the Warring States (475-221 BCE). It was regarded by most scholars as the *Huangdi Neijing* (*Inner Canon of the Yellow Emperor*) but this was a collection of various forms of different texts, rather like a compilation. It underwent changes throughout subsequent years. The first book ever written in Chinese history was produced in the Han Dynasty (202-220 BCE) containing the descriptions and uses of exactly 365 Chinese herbal extracts in medicine. One of the most legendary doctors in China was called Hua Tuo, also in the Han Dynasty, who was regarded as extraordinarily proficient in the use of herbal extracts for diseases and who also practised anaesthesia, acupuncture, and even some forms of surgery. In comparison, the origin and the foundation of Western medicine was generally attributed to Greece with the physician known as Hippocrates of Cos (460-370 BCE) who was regarded as the Father of Western Medicine. His Hippocratic Oath was and still is the universal code of practice for the medical profession. Yet, compared with TCM, Western medicine had a very young history in China. It was thought that it was introduced into China first in the 16th century by the Jesuit missionaries, possibly through the then Portuguese colony called Macao in the South China Sea, though it was never quite accepted by the Chinese people then. The real emergence and acceptance of Western medicine was from the middle of the 19th century after the Opium War when missionaries, many of them were qualified doctors, started to come to China. Since then, Western medicine has become the dominant medicine accepted by most of the Chinese people.

It is very hard for me as a non-TCM-trained doctor to describe or explain the theory behind TCM. It deals with balances, equilibrium, and inner energy (called *Qi*) and makes observations on the patient and tries to redress the balance by use of herbal extracts or manoeuvres such as acupuncture through designated points, based on traditional meridians in the body. In the last few decades, some real groundbreaking therapeutic breakthroughs were also made by TCM. The most famous of these is the cure of a special but fatal type of leukaemia known as acute promyelocytic leukaemia, based on the experience and practice of TCM. TCM also pioneered one of the most recent forms of malarial treatment, or the treatment of some dermatological diseases. The other contribution of TCM is the science and practice of acupuncture, which is now very popular globally, widely practised by both professional acupuncturists and some anaesthesiologists. All of these have won international awards, recognition, and credibility. In China, TCM must be offered as a clinical service in any 3A hospitals, with both inpatient and outpatient facilities.

Initially, this was a problem for us to set up TCM service at HKU SZH, as the presence of TCM was not part of the original hospital design. I have already mentioned the conversion of what was originally designed as the intravenous infusion area to a TCM outpatient area while a ward was also created for inpatient TCM service. But how do we integrate TCM with Western medicine? Those of us who practise Western medicine all base our skills and knowledge on basic pharmacological and physiological training. When we prescribe a drug, not only we must know its uses and its licensed indications, we must also know the common side effects. Knowing one without knowing the other is a substandard or unsafe practice. Equally, a surgical procedure will not be carried out without patients knowing the likely post-operative complications. I know next to nothing about TCM and feel that I am simply not qualified to formulate an informed view on this, especially on the use of herbal extracts as some form of medical therapy. With the medications that the patient may already be on, caution is always needed when one is to prescribe an additional medication.

The problem therefore is that in TCM, none of these core issues are really scientifically well documented and studied in its practice. It is essentially based on experience passed down through generations, with no major scientific data on how it works, why it works, and the likely side effects, not to mention toxicity. I am not for one minute negating the use of TCM but rather proposing that there is a need for a degree of caution and realism in the practice of it. Safety is the key and our motto should be to do no harm. I myself have often been asked by patients and their relatives on the need or the advisability for the concurrent use of Chinese medicines as an adjunct to a standardised regimen of chemotherapy. My answer to them has always been that I am a Western-trained doctor and as such I am totally unfamiliar with TCM. Therefore, in all honesty I cannot really pass a professional opinion on its use. I would also add that I am concerned about the real question of drug interaction in either augmenting or reducing the efficacy of concurrent Western-based treatment. Thus, my advice to them is not to use TCM when the patient is under my care. Just in case, when untoward side effects do happen, one will find it very difficult to ascertain if it is the Western medication or the Chinese medicine that is the culprit. One can only be held accountable to what one prescribes and not to what one does not prescribe. I am very pleased and relieved the patients, without exception, accept my explanation and advice.

It is also important to emphasise that Western medicine and TCM should not be exclusive of each other, rather, it can help to increase the clinical scope for each other. Time is needed for this integration which requires careful scientific and clinical studies. The practice of acupuncture is already very much part of Western medicine and equally some practice of TCM has included forms of Western medicine such as antibiotics and analgesics.

CHAPTER 15

Access to Drugs

This has been a problem in China, especially in the field of modern new anticancer drugs, which took me quite a while to get used to. Initially I often felt my scope of treating the patients with haematological problems was rather restricted. Some drugs, which have been in use widely over the last 30 years, are not available in China as they do not have a licence. The reasons can either be that the manufacturer deems that it is not commercially viable to apply for a new licence for a traditional drug in China as an old drug may be difficult to market and hence, the profit margin may be too small. This is a commercial decision. The other reason is that the drug may be so new that licensing of these new drugs often takes a long time and has to go through layers of applications and processes. For me, it is a source of regret that these drugs were not available in China, as some of them could be lifesaving.

To get around this problem in China, the clinicians would tell the patient a certain drug is needed but not available in China, though used and proven useful clinically outside China. The onus is therefore on the part of the patients to get these drugs. The patients and the families will then demonstrate remarkable ingenuity and resourcefulness in getting these drugs, often through either travelling to Hong Kong or even paying unapproved agents who can procure these drugs via Hong Kong, at a premium of course. These agents may or may not be medically qualified. Where there is a will, there is a way. The problem with this is that this process is not properly validated, and one cannot be sure if the drug is the genuine product or not. For my own practice at HKU SZH, since I do also have a Hong Kong practising licence as I am an HKU graduate, I will write out a proper prescription, by special arrangement and approval by the hospital senior management, for a certain drug to be dispensed in Hong Kong. So at least this process is open and accountable, and a detailed traceable record is kept.

The other option is to shop around in the black-market copies of these drugs, often made in India, at a cheaper though still significant price. In fact, this second option was so widely used that the controversial and ethical issues involved in this were made into a film in China in 2018. This film received huge public attention. I watched the film too. It was about the life story of a leukaemia patient needing a life-saving drug, licensed in China, imported from overseas, but very expensive. The cheaper version of this drug was made and available in India. This cheaper version was a copycat version and unlicensed. In the film, the patient had to go to India to get the India-made generic but unlicensed overseas version. Two weeks after the release of this film 'Dying to Survive', China's Prime Minister, Mr Li Keqiang, made a public comment and urged regulators to get new cancer drugs for national approval more quickly and at lower prices too.

Fake drugs or obtaining expensive drugs via the black market through illegal drug syndicates can be a major problem. This is now being heavily clamped down by the government with significant success. Some people I meet would say to me this is a social phenomenon and a necessary growing pain in any developing country, as patients can be very desperate in getting what they need. I often explained to them that this desperation, understandable though it may be, will make them very vulnerable to being cheated or exploited. This would be one of the worst kinds of human behaviour as one is cheating and trading on the lives of the ills in society.

However, the situation has improved in the last two years. In fact, this marked improvement may be related to the popular film mentioned previously about going to India for copy drugs which are usually much cheaper. It highlighted the difficulties that the patients face with new and expensive life-saving drugs. The government clearly recognised that there is a need to be met and a gap to be filled. This film was timely in a way that it made the issue more topical and the central government took decisive actions. The approval for licence for drugs is run by CFDA (China Food and Drug Administration), and the process of approval is now much quicker. There is also a fast-track mechanism, much like in the USA and European Union. In the past, I would have to issue a prescription for our patients to take to Hong Kong where it would be dispensed. The need for this was averaging about twice a month, but now I have not needed to do so in the last 12 months. This laudable improvement, together with a policy of national procurement in driving down the price (just like in the UK), not only makes many of these new drugs available, but also the price can actually be cheaper than in Hong Kong. The direct beneficiaries are the patients, reducing the need for them travelling to Hong Kong and avoiding the cost of paying the middle agents in getting access to these drugs. On this particular aspect, I can safely predict things will continue to improve. In other words, new drugs will be available in China much quicker than before and cheaper too.

China is now also investing heavily in cutting-edge modern technology in the production of new drugs, especially anticancer drugs and cellular immuno-therapies. This homegrown industry's makeover was initiated by the growing alignment of China's drug regulations with international standards. Huge investments have been made in the last few years. In 2018, the sales of drugs in China reached USD137 billion, second in the world and will reach half of the US spend by 2030, while currently it is about a quarter. So there is huge room for expansion and development. Much of the sales of these new drugs will then not be from imports but domestically produced. China's drug makers, while traditionally have been producing cheap copycat drugs for domestic use, have now moved up the skill ladder to make innovative new drugs and cellular products too. These new home-made products, manufactured in line with international standards, will also likely enter, at some stage, the international competitive market too. In addition, because of the huge patient base, many global top pharmaceutical companies are also actively engaging the Chinese medical profession as principal investigators in clinical trials and basic studies. This will be discussed in Chapter 24.

CHAPTER 16

Principles in the Pricing and Charging of Services in Shenzhen

This section discusses the principles of pricing of services and the local government medical insurance scheme in Shenzhen. This model is equally applicable to the rest of China as the national government is aiming in the long term to set up a standardised scheme throughout the country, even though currently the local government medical insurance scheme may vary from region to region.

The Complexities of Costings and Charges

Every item of services has a fixed price which is published by the local government and public hospitals can only charge for these services at this fixed price. When I first arrived in HKU SZH, one of the first things I was given to study was a price list which I called the *Green Book*. This book has been my constant companion, night and day, placed right in the centre of my desk. The *Green Book* now has been updated to include 9,412 items of services chargeable at fixed price for itemised billing. The range of these items is staggering, from the price of a simple blood test to the most sophisticated operation, from the prescription of a simple bedside monitor to the use of a ventilator in the Intensive Care Unit (ICU). This *Green Book* is therefore the rule book serving as a price list for tests, treatments, drugs, procedures, or operations in Shenzhen for the public hospitals. For example, if I wish to start a service like thrombolytic therapy for strokes, I need to work out in detail the costs and the chargeable price involved in each of the necessary steps such as CT scanning, the drugs, and the stent being used. So even though this *Green Book* does have an electronic version available on the local government website for reference, I was still much attached to its print copy. When I first came to Shenzhen, I knew nothing then. My understanding of Chinese terminology for items of services was very poor and so I had to keep referring to it, not only as a source of pricing but more as a source of learning too. So, for the first two years, it was my permanent reading companion on the desk, within reach, especially in the evenings. No other books came close!

The hospital IT system is set up in such a way that every instruction or request a doctor wishes to issue, such as a bedside cardiac monitor, or use of a drug and a blood test, could only be carried out upon the generation of an IT request, which will then automatically price each as a chargeable item and will add up the daily running total of charges based on these fixed prices, just like shopping with a basket of items and then paying via an Amazon website.

The payment for such services by the patients will depend on if he/she will be self-financing or has Shenzhen government insurance scheme which will reimburse a portion of the fees for consultations with doctors, the prescribed medications, diagnostic tests, or surgical equipment. The same principle applies to both the OPD and inpatient services. For major and chronic illness such as cancer, chronic renal failure, and post-transplant care, both in and outpatient charges can be covered up to 90% if the patient has more than three years of Shenzhen insurance. For those short-term migrant workers without government insurance, they can also claim a percentage of total charge based on the cover of the area of residence from where they come from. I have always said to my British and Chinese friends that, in my opinion, the Shenzhen government insurance scheme provides one of the most comprehensive, modern, and reasonable insurance covers that I have ever experienced. The residents in Shenzhen should definitely be encouraged to buy into the scheme.

However, such is the complexity of modern healthcare that even this *Green Book*, as detailed as it is, is not regarded as comprehensive enough. I don't think there is in existence anywhere in any medical institution which can come up with a comprehensive and updated price list for every single item of service. Price lists for items of service need to be constantly reviewed and updated, just like a well-stocked modern supermarket, except in healthcare, it is much more complicated. Unlike the supermarkets where the customer decides what is needed to be purchased, in the medical services it is usually the provider, i.e. the doctor, who decides what services are needed, such as diagnostic blood tests and other investigations. The provision or the appropriateness of a medical opinion given by a doctor cannot always be quantified, so even though each item is priced, the total charge may vary from patient to patient.

It is also likely that no sooner the *Green Book* is updated and published, there will be items of services which need to be added on. This is the unavoidable nature of the practice of medicine. In Shenzhen, every year the health officials will ask if there are services which need to be added as a chargeable item. Any such application will be initially coordinated by our Finance Department, with various professional inputs and the costs worked out in detail. After submission, the Shenzhen government would then start a very detailed and comprehensive process in assessing the needs of this new service and a detailed validation of the cost-effectiveness. The applicants will be invited to attend various meetings to put forward the case. There will be different members forming various panels to scrutinise the applications. Once the request is granted, then it will be applicable to all hospitals. I had the personal experience of going through the process of applying for our haematopoietic stem cells harvesting and storage (cryopreservation) as an integral and chargeable part of our haematopoietic stem cell transplant services, and after nearly a year, our application was approved. The benefit for this is that it is not only chargeable at HKU SZH, it can also be used in other hospitals that wish to establish a similar service in Shenzhen. If, after a year, more hospitals are developing this service, then it would be actively considered to be included in the government insurance scheme which will mean that this chargeable service will become a claimable service.

I found this exercise very useful as it does give us a chance to develop some new service, which will be properly cost first, assessed fairly and thoroughly by a team of experts. Once approved and established, then other hospitals can also set up this service where there is a clinical need. Equally, this process can also provide an opportunity in which some old and antiquated services can be considered for decommissioning. This mechanism ensures that any new service is primarily clinically driven while the management, especially the finance department, plays a key role in costing and supporting the application process.

Just like the commercial insurance for buildings, houses, travelling or car, there will still be exclusion items which are not covered. It is also similar in the healthcare sector in China, as in most other countries. For the items of service (e.g. new drugs) that are not covered, it does mean that patients have to self-finance such services, in which case, there is a standard practice that the patient or the families be informed about this self-financing item and an informed consent is required and signed for. This is a day-to-day practice such as in my own field of haematology in which new chemotherapies are often quite expensive. Consent to pay for self-financing items is absolutely essential in the system as it can help to prevent any future disputes or disgruntlement.

A Personal Experience

To explain the charging process, I have a personal first-hand experience which I would like to share with the readers. A few years ago, a very dear relative of mine needed a major operation, and she chose to come to HKU SZH for the operation. She is not a Shenzhen resident, she is from Hong Kong, so she had to pay for the treatment because she does not have Shenzhen government insurance though she was entitled to a free service in Hong Kong in the public sector. So, she had to sign the consent form for payment and paid a deposit. She stayed as an inpatient for 14 days during which every day I, as her close relative, was given a list of the tests or service provided and the running total of the charges, so I knew exactly the cost of the surgery, anaesthesia, the medications, and the tests, and on her discharge, the total cost was paid, minus the deposit. The most interesting thing was that half-way through, when the deposit nearly went out, I was asked to top up the deposit, to reduce the loss to the hospital in the event of non-payment. On mature reflection, I thought this was a very fair and transparent system because it gave me a day-to-day account of what had been done and charged, and indeed, just like paying for a restaurant meal, you know exactly what you are paying for, item by item. This is a good demonstration of knowing the price of something that is done and also knowing the value of something and in this case, the value of an operation with a successful outcome. Patients and their relatives can check and raise any query if they so wish. The other advantage is that it gives the patient a feel of the resources required to run a medical service, with a detailed breakdown to even the price of each individual medication. Being cost-conscious by both the providers and users of health services is a very important aspect of healthcare. It enables them to be much more aware of the precious resources needed for any healthcare system. In a system like the NHS in the UK, where the funding is underwritten by the government, cost consciousness does not appear in the mind of the users (patients) though it is always on the minds of the providers (doctors and managers). There is a schism there.

From time to time, there will be some situations where patients cannot afford any treatment for a life-threatening disease. This is a very difficult area in which ethics, humanities, and affordability are important issues to be considered, particularly in a system where each hospital has to balance its books on a yearly basis. There is unfortunately no perfect solution to this. Our hospital is of the view that ethics and humanities come first, and for services provided in our Emergency Room, no patients can be refused. The hospital also has a charitable fund set aside for this reason, and the use of this fund is considered on a case-by-case basis by the senior executives. Our Finance Department also keeps a regular and updated list of such non-paying patients, to be used in our regular discussion with local government healthcare officials.

The other new pricing mechanism HKU SZH has introduced into China is the use of package charge for a well-defined procedure or operation such as laparoscopic cholecystectomy. What the hospital did was to collect information of the total charges for each patient using data collected from large numbers of patients over the years and, with the active input of the Finance Department, work out an average package charge for the whole operation, from admission to discharge, without having to charge for each item of service. Active discussion then followed with the local government health care officials. With their approval, there are now more than 20 procedures and surgeries, all accurately identifiable by ICD 10 coding, for which package charges are in place and implemented since 2015. Feedback from the patients and the government has been excellent and encouraging. The package charge, applicable to both insured and self-finance patients, while complicated to work out initially, is easy to understand and implement, much like going for a buffet dinner! I am positive and optimistic that this package charge will expand, thus bringing in another change to Shenzhen and beyond.

Are Our Charges Competitive?

I often get asked by my friends and colleagues in Hong Kong and the UK the following: are the medical services in China cheaper compared with the system in Hong Kong or the UK? There are, in my view, two aspects to this important but searching question: First, in China, the staff are much more price conscious, even in public hospitals, and the doctors are exceptionally well-informed about prices. If they are not sure, they can always check the price from any computer anywhere in the hospital. It is the standard way the system works in China and it is one of the main drivers in running a hospital. This is totally different from the UK or Hong Kong where the doctors are generally not well-informed about the costs, let alone price, except in the private sector, where both the hospital and the doctors know the price of everything which is chargeable. The other view that I will always give them is that: yes, it is much cheaper in China. My own estimate is that it can vary from 10% to almost 90% cheaper, depending on the nature of the service, such as drugs provided, or surgery performed. Once this question is answered, then there will be predictably another immediate follow-up question: is the standard equally good? What about clinical competence? Service standards and clinical competence are clearly what a hospital is about, and this will be further addressed in Chapter 20.

CHAPTER 17

Medical Complaints, Disputes, and Violence

Before I came back to China, some concerned friends and colleagues had advised me against my decision to take up the offer at HKU SZH for fear of the problem of medical violence. This violence was often reported in the national press, but also widely discussed in the international medical press, even in highly respected peer-reviewed journals. I had not experienced this medical violence in my years in the UK, and so I asked myself: What is medical violence in China? For me, it can be regarded as a wilful act of someone who carries out physical harm, premeditated or spontaneous, to another person. This other person is mainly one of the medical or nursing staff, and the people who carry out the act can be a single person such as the patient or someone from the families, in the premises of the hospital. The means of this harm can be a punch, a kick, or a push and worse still, a weapon such as a wooden stick or a knife, though never ever firearms as firearms are outlawed, rightfully in my views, in China. Occasionally, fatalities had been reported in these acts of violence, usually from knife wounds to the doctors. One can hardly imagine what the scenario could be if firearms are not outlawed. I have indeed come across some threatened acts of both verbal and physical abuse when I first arrived.

So what are the reasons for complaints, disputes, and even violence? There are several possible reasons: monetary, failures in communication, lack of understanding of the nature of medical care, inappropriate information from the internet, and genuine mistakes.

How Can We Tackle this Complicated Issue?

I have no unique wisdom or insight here, but I would like to offer some views. The first is that patients expect what they perceive as the right kind of medical care on offer and what kind of outcome such care will bring. With the astounding success in China in leaping from one of the poorest but largest countries to the dizzy level of being the world's second largest economy, the success it brings, especially in tackling poverty, can equally cloud our judgements or perceptions of the true meaning of prosperity, and in particular the difference between prosperity and civility. In striving for this economic success, a tendency is developed into a prevailing desire to make money and be competitive. There is, however, an obvious downside to this desire, which is that every human interaction involving payments can then be viewed as a possible form of commercial transaction. The money I pay for the service needs to be reflected in the outcome of the service much like other consumer services, such as the style of the haircut by the hairdresser, or the tastiness of the food served in the restaurant. This is the 'value for service' concept. But what is the meaning of the word value here? Is it a figure? Or is the value linked with the outcome and so, if the outcome is not perfect, can it mean less value? And does lower price mean less value? There is of course nothing intrinsically wrong with this generic 'value for service' concept as this will drive the motivation for improvement on the part of the provider for the benefit of the customers or the patients.

Yet, the practice of medicine is far from being a commercial transaction based on a monetary figure for a drug or a procedure or a service. This is a totally different concept to buying a consumer product which comes with a guarantee of at least a year, and if broken or defective, a replacement or a refund can be forthcoming. Medicine involves trust by both parties and the principle of its practice, just as life itself, is that nothing can be guaranteed. It is not possible to achieve 100% success and a guaranteed outcome, freed from any side effects. The patients and the families must be aware of this, which forms the whole basis of informed consent. All practices in medicine are based on clinical training over a long period of time. This is to ensure that adequate experience is acquired in offering the correct clinical opinions, and the implementation of treatment, which can vary from patient to patient, such as which drug to use in a mild case of hypertension as opposed to severe and unresponsive hypertension. The relative risks of an emergency life-saving operation as opposed to an elective non-life-threatening surgery are all variable factors in this complex matrix. So, while a well-intentioned, professional service is offered, the outcome is never guaranteed. And yet a consultation process, be it in medical opinions or performance of a surgery, will involve a fee paid for by the patient, even with the cover of state medical insurance. Once payment is involved, then there is the perception of this being a commercial transaction, a trade so to speak. As such, a less than perfect outcome, just like a faulty consumer product, there is a tendency to ask for a replacement or a refund. Everything is viewed by some as a trade! But medicine is not a trade, it is about dealing with an ailment of a patient.

In medicine, any patient who has a suboptimal treatment outcome can generally have the following responses: to accept that treatment may not always work and may have side effects, and an alternative treatment can be sought; to surmise that the treatment is suboptimal and view this as a human error and thus has every right to seek compensation, or worse still, to vent their anger or disappointment in the form of physical violence on the perceived culprits. In my view, all the above responses are possible but seeking compensation and resorting to violence seemed to be particularly common in China and for reasons which I have explained above.

Any conflicts involve two sides. A medical complaint or dispute may also be the fault of the doctor. Apart from viewing a treatment for a medical condition as a financial transaction in which a less-than-optimal performance can be refunded, the other main reason for disputes is the lack of empathy shown by the doctor to the patient. On this issue alone much more needs to be done by the medical profession. In fact, I would venture to say this is actually the main cause of medical disputes and perhaps the easiest and cheapest to resolve. Often inadequate effort is made to explain to the patient and the families. Communication and explaining with empathy are core parts of our job. We serve the patients with our professionalism which involves empathy, compassion, as well as our clinical knowledge. Regrettably, such essential qualities are quite intangible. The cost of these cannot be measured as it involves the attitude of and the proper communication by the doctors. These are not chargeable as a service item, and they are certainly not in the *Green Book* described in the previous chapter. Because it is not chargeable, there is no incentive to do so and thus the need for proper communication is often ignored. As doctors are often paid according to how many patients they see, how many items of drugs they prescribe, or how many surgeries or procedures they perform, their basic incomes can often be augmented by extra clinical activities with bonuses. This principle of increasing income by seeing more and doing more of course is prevalent in industries, which want to sell more and more, but this cannot be effectively or indeed should not be applied to medical services. The users of this service are patients, who often come with question marks and with great anxiety. They need and deserve a proper explanation and reassurance. This anxiety is often not appreciated or dealt with by the doctors (lack of empathy), hence, later leading to complaints and disputes when things go wrong.

Therefore, proper communication is vital in preventing complaints or disputes. It is often pointed out that in China, the doctors simply would not have the time to spend on explaining to the patients in any meaningful or helpful manner. They are overwhelmed by the sheer number of patients needed to be seen.

At HKU SZH, we view it as a matter of top priority the importance of the concept of patient-centred service in which one of the key areas is to improve communication, to explain and to reassure. Complaints often made are because of patients and families who are not entirely clear of what is happening and thus they would be anxious, as we all would if we were patients. I have always taught our staff and students that people's reactions to ailments can be both predictable and unpredictable, and empathy is one of the best ways to smooth this out while apathy will have the exact opposite effect. Proper communication is never a one-off event but rather a daily event, especially in medicine, when patients' conditions may or may not improve, drug dosages may be changed. So effective communication is needed throughout the whole of the patient journey in the hospital and this is a key service provision that we have introduced and required from our staff at HKU SZH right from the beginning.

The other major reform that HKU SZH introduced was to launch a zero-tolerance policy to medical violence. This is a brave and far-sighted project, a project which has now received national support and endorsement, copied already by many other hospitals. This zero-tolerance policy is fully supported by the local government and the police. Notices are widely displayed in the hospital of this policy and widely shared with the media as well. Whatever the grievances, violence cannot be condoned and must be avoided at all costs.

At the national level, it is my own observation that this trend of acts of violence and the prevalence of medical disputes have already received attention by the top officials in the central government. New instructions have been circulated to local governments and actions are now taken both by the law enforcement agencies and hospitals for implementation. Civil penalties would be issued for offenders. The new social credit system only recently introduced in China may improve this situation further.

The other reason is a modern phenomenon. It is a by-product of the modern internet age, where information or misinformation can be instantly sought and accessed at any moment. We have an illness, we receive the treatment, we then check on the net and cross-check if the treatment is right. We have all, to various extents, become netizens! This is the plus of the internet; it offers the chance of alternative and instant information. The problem is that information on the internet is not subject to regulation, so much of the information can be based on hearsay or exaggeration. The Internet gives us information, though not necessarily knowledge. Because this information superhighway is often funded by advertising revenue, it can therefore often be a source for exaggerated, misleading, or erroneous information. This is especially prevalent in blog-based chatting forums, where opinions expressed are nearly always personal, judgemental, subjective, or even condemning, rather than sensible and impartial. The undiscerning patient can form a view on what he/she reads, concludes that he/she may be mismanaged and then proceeds to question and complain, perhaps even with the ulterior motive of having their paid treatment refunded. In short, the complaints or grievances can be justified or not justified. I personally welcome comments and would not shy away from having complaints, which I have always taken seriously, as they offer me the chance to hear the other side of the story and improve our service.

The final reason is that a genuine mistake is made, or an untoward incident occurs. It goes without saying that it is right and proper when a genuine mistake is made, not only should it be admitted and apologised for but also the question of compensation needs to be addressed. At HKU SZH, there is a special, highly visible Patient Relation Office (PRO) in the atrium of the central block of our hospital that deals with complaints or grievances. Once a complaint is received, it will be logged on the database. The staff can then initiate a speedy process of investigations, with meetings held weekly, chaired by a senior doctor, to come up with action, solutions, or explanations to the patients. No complaints will be ignored. Data and records are comprehensively collected, analysed, and stored, conversations with the patients and families are taped, subject to their approval. Where wrongdoings and mistakes are confirmed, an official apology and an appropriate compensation will be offered.

One notable initiative that HKU SZH undertook is to buy a collective indemnity scheme for all the staff from an insurance company, much like the crown indemnity in the UK or the Hospital Authority (which runs all the public hospitals) backed indemnity in Hong Kong. We have a hospital liability and not an individual staff liability. Any compensation, so decided by a tribunal or a hospital committee, in consultation with our legal representatives, will be paid out by the insurance company and not an individual. It needs to be pointed out in China, many such financial settlements are paid out by the hospitals themselves and not insurance companies and furthermore, this will also lead to a financial penalty on the doctors or nurses who made the mistake.

With all our collective efforts described above, made diligently and steadfastly, over the past few years by both the hospital and the local government, along with the huge efforts in public education, it is very rewarding to state that complaints or disputes are now much less common. There is also a marked drop in medical violence, not only in our hospital but in China too. Things are definitely moving in the right direction.

CHAPTER 18

The Use of Red Packets

To understand the practice of giving red packets, one needs to know the traditional significance for its use. The colour red signifies good fortune, happiness, and liveliness in Chinese culture. So, for any celebrations such as a traditional Chinese wedding, the brides wear red costumes and in Chinese New Year, most decorations such as calligraphic posters for good wishes are all written on pieces of red poster. The dancing dragons displayed in Chinese New Year are also in red. The red packets (designed like small envelopes) usually contain some paper money inside, of various amounts. They are usually given out on special occasions from the old to the young, on birthdays, weddings, the Chinese New Year, or any other occasions calling for celebration as a good luck blessing.

This idea of giving out red packets as blessing can also serve as an expression of affection and appreciation (I was once given a red packet for passing an examination by my uncle), much like the modern Western practice of giving a shopping token for Apple or Amazon around Christmas time or if a student passes an examination. The amount of cash inside is flexible and there is no standard amount for any special occasions. This is more flexible than the use of an Amazon coupon which has a certain degree of restriction. So the idea of giving a red packet is based on good intentions and indeed, my wife, who is English, loves giving out red packets not only during Chinese New Year, but also for birthdays or wedding celebrations or even Christmas in the UK to both our Chinese and British friends. They have always appreciated this gesture. In fact, the first time she received a red packet was during our traditional Chinese wedding ceremony when, following the traditional Chinese practice, she knelt down and served my mother a cup of Chinese tea, whereupon my mother gave her a red packet as a blessing. She was delighted by this traditional symbolic gesture.

All good practice or traditions, however, can also be abused or misused, especially if the cash inside is of a large amount. Its misuse, in my opinion, can be defined as follows:

The secret transfer of gains from one stakeholder to another, direct or indirect, can be subtle (like promotion of career), secretive (like the use of a car or hotel resort), uncheckable (like hosting of a lavish dinner banquet), or cash (large amount in a red packet). These gains are not available to other stakeholders who are therefore unknowingly disadvantaged.

Those receiving such gain can be a single person or a group of people forming a syndicate. In other words, such a practice can be syndicated too. In the healthcare sector in China, it is often used as a secret means of courting special favours for treatment by a famous specialist through offering extra cash, which can be a large amount. These favours can also vary from a fast tracking appointment to see a famous specialist, designation of a preferred surgeon to perform a specific operation, the prescription of expensive drugs, or expensive equipment from a certain supplier, or the prescription of expensive drugs not for personal use, but to be re-sold in the black market at a profit. So the rules of the system have been bent illegally for personal gain, especially hidden financial gain.

I think it is important here to point out that this 'hidden cash for privileges' is not a phenomenon unique or originating in China. Far from it. It is an age-old practice, even as old as ancient Rome. For instance, it is a centuries-old practice for the formation of brotherhood societies or professional guilds. The aim was to enhance standards and promote comradeship, but it could also be used to establish connections, patronage, and favouritism, so people outside the system would be unknowingly disadvantaged. In the modern world, the practice is called lobbying or networking, involving donation or payment, for political influence, or for a decision favourable to those who pay for the lobbying. This may be legal but often there is a very fine line between what is and what is not legal. This means the methods these lobbyists employ can be opaque, or even dark indeed. Even in what are known as democratic and open societies, there are oblique ways of transferring financial interests in paying for influences such as a donation to a political party or an established organisation. From time to time in the UK, there are accusations in the press about peerages for sale, or even illegal commission paid to the relative of a political figure in securing arms deals. This particular form of buying for influence is especially noticeable during an election campaign in some countries.

This is not in any way condoning the use of red packet is hospital practice in China but is an effort to explain that such acts of giving something of value in return for favours is very much part of human nature and a social phenomenon. Just because we see things done as an acceptable common practice in society, it does not mean these things are inevitably right or cannot be abused, especially if the motive behind such acts are distorted for personal gain. It certainly does not mean it is acceptable for the medical profession to engage in the same practice. It is about professional ethics and setting a boundary beyond which we must not cross, especially the people we serve are patients who need us to help them, red packets or not.

So it is up to us, the practitioners and providers of services, to ensure fairness. Over the last few years, the Chinese government has made significant strides in tackling this problem of corruption, making it a national priority. At HKU SZH, it has been our open and stated policy right from Day 1 that our hospital will not allow the staff to accept red packets nor engage in any back channels to receive any non-accountable financial rewards. Here, our practice is that doctors and patients co-sign an agreement on admission to forbid the giving and receiving of red packets and any breach of this agreement can lead to disciplinary action or even dismissal. This practice, when first introduced, was widely applauded and seen as a key and bold plank of our reforms. It is unclear though if other hospitals have similar reforms, though I suspect it may be difficult for them to do so. Habits, especially the long-held ones, can be difficult to change. It takes time. Old habits die hard but change we must.

CHAPTER 19

Bonus Culture

I have always supported the practice of awarding bonuses as an extra means of rewarding and appreciating those dedicated and committed staff who work in the healthcare system. It is a bit like share options in a private enterprise. It serves very well to incentivise the staff to enhance productivity and if used properly, there is no loser and is a classic win-win situation. This is why it is universally adopted by many organisations.

However, on looking deeper, I feel that the use of bonus cannot be seen as a replacement for a fair basic pay in any employment. Salary should be determined by the values and the nature of skills required for a specific job. Therefore, the job should also have the proper remuneration value attached to it. Unlike in the case of a relatively untrained sales assistant in a shop, whose basic pay may be low but can be supplemented by bonus if the sales figures increase. This model of remuneration may not be appropriate to apply to the medical profession. First, it takes years of learning to be qualified for such a profession and secondly, we are told that our job is to help the sick, an honest day's work for an honest day's pay, with a basic salary in line with how society thinks we deserve. In China, the general pay of healthcare professionals tends to be low, compared to other countries, and yet the pressures faced by the doctors can be much higher for reasons which I have already discussed in the previous chapters. Unlike many other countries, where the doctors' pay in the public sector is generally fixed with a national standard on a pay spine, the salary of a doctor in China can be negotiated before commencement of duty. Furthermore, the pay for an entry-level doctor can be low, such as a few thousand RMB per month. Because of the lack of standard, a benchmark cannot be established with the net result that the take-home pay for doctors can vary from person to person, department to department, hospital to hospital, and region to region. For each hospital, there will be a need and a must for various forms of bonuses to incentivise the staff to have a take-home salary at an acceptable and attractive level. The challenge is how to ensure a transparent, open, and fair standard for the distribution of the bonuses. It is human nature for us to think we all work very hard compared with our colleagues and as such we deserve more. One of the areas that HKU SZH pioneered when we first started in 2012 was to have a standard salary structure where structured pay and conditions are the standards while bonuses can best be regarded as a token of recognition of extra efforts.

Anomaly in the UK

This principle of rewarding doctors with bonuses may have another downside too. In the UK, there is a similar bonus system known as a national award system. I have personally seen the pitfalls in this, and I would like to describe the pitfalls in some detail here. This national award system is called the Clinical Excellence Awards, administered yearly by the Advisory Committee on Clinical Excellence Awards (ACCEA). These awards are available only to consultants and professors. The idea is to reward those who work over and above what they are contracted for. This award is not standardised and is classified into platinum, gold, silver, and bronze awards. There lies the problem, the amount so awarded in the highest award, called the platinum award, can be as high as the annual salary of the award holder, who is usually already a very senior clinician contributing to national or international work. Most likely too, he or she may already be on the top of the pay scale. So the more well-connected and involved one is in some sort of advisory role in national committees or international institutions, the more likely one is to be given a higher award. The highest award effectively means that it can double the take home pay for the award holder and this award is pensionable too. The award, unlike bonus, is given for five years and is renewable. Furthermore, no other professions allied to medicine working in a hospital have such an award system. This does therefore create a perception of privileges for the few. It attracts much criticism and generates much resentment especially among the younger doctors, not to mention other professions within the health service. The perverse logic, therefore, viewed by some, is that hard work in seeing patients does not count, while connections with national institutions do count! Time spent away from the hospital can bring more potential financial rewards than time spent in the hospital. In my view, it would have been much more acceptable if the merit award was weighted more on the merits of the clinical work with less emphasis on the actual monetary value, or else it will be, wrongly or rightly, seen as a pursuit of money with the wrong motive. Senior, dedicated doctors do good work for its own sake, the award of money should be a secondary consideration at best. Therefore, the reward of an excessive amount of money can distort the incentive.

In China, extra work, merits, or contributions are rewarded as bonuses which are given yearly. The main area of contention, the way I see it, is that the basic salary for healthcare workers is low, unlike in other major economies, and thus the use of bonus can help the staff to significantly boost the take-home income. So, in the minds of the staff, their personal financial planning will inevitably need to be based on salary and bonus. Most public hospitals in China have to have a balanced budget each year, with an average that 85% of their revenue has to come from the hospital's clinical activities. Government support is much less compared with places like Hong Kong or the UK. So for any hospital, the financial balance is always dependent on income generated. More patients seen and treated, more tests and procedures carried out, more drugs prescribed will bring in more income and the income has to have a surplus before any bonus can be shared with the staff. So the net effect is that when staff work in this system of bonus awarded on activities, they will invariably develop a 'More is Good' (more bonus), 'Less is Bad' (less income) mindset in fulfilling their clinical duties. They will be motivated to drive up activities which can be counted but less inclined to drive up quality which is much more difficult to measure.

In the commercial world, this financial viability is measured through analysing the matrix of productivity, efficiency, turnover, and growth. However, in a public hospital, where income generation is based on such a principle of balancing the expenditure, which includes the payment of bonuses, it is therefore quite legitimate to ask: will the emphasis on increased activity to generate more income be at the expense of compromising on quality, safety, and above all, time on communication with patients and their families? The irony here is: The more I see, the more I get but the more I explain, the less I get. Thus, the doctors in this system will have an incentive to see as many patients as possible and tend to avoid those patients with complicated medical problems as a means of boosting up the productivity. This may be the downside. Quantity of work maximises revenue while quality of work may not. At HKU SZH, the yearly bonus is not only measured by activity but also by other indicators such as punctuality in attending clinics, proper documentation of case notes, active participation in accreditation exercises, audits, and complaints. In other words, we try to include some tangible quality data as the basis of working out bonuses. The idea here is to strike a balance between patient safety, quality of care, governance, and workload. It is graded in nature and is capped, but the amount is not as excessive as the system in the UK.

Therefore, I think this bonus culture on the whole is positive and should be encouraged, particularly since it is available to all staff, unlike the UK system, which is only available to consultants and professors. The way to improve it further is to ensure that quality and safety are structurally built into the assessment system to award bonuses which, if used properly, transparently and fairly, can really help to encourage and motivate staff. At HKU SZH, much work has already been done in this respect to ensure fairness and openness. This was once light-heartedly, jokingly, and affectionately described by some mainland colleagues as a 'sunshine income', meaning openness and visible, not murky nor grey! I was quite pleased when I heard this.

CHAPTER 20

Clinical Competence and Expertise

It is common for people, not least the patients, to wonder if the doctors they see are clinically competent. Is he/she up to standard? Does he/she keep up with the latest information? Does he/she have the right experience? Does he/she look too old (past the sell-by date) or too young (inexperienced)? These are completely legitimate concerns anywhere in the world and, in fact, failure to wonder about this means we are not behaving in a way we should as patients. Trusting a doctor is one thing but blind trust is altogether different. We as doctors do make mistakes. The world may not be perfect, and we doctors certainly are not.

So how can I answer this question? In my eight years of clinical practice in China, it is my conclusion that the medical workforce is highly competent, especially in the major 3A hospitals. Their knowledge is extremely updated, they are nearly always familiar with the latest international or national guidelines and their practical skills such as surgical or procedural skills are on par with other major countries in the world such as the USA, the UK, or Europe. The acquisition of such skills and experience has much to do with the large number of often clinically challenging and interesting case mixes. Over a short period of time, and with a high number of cases, the acquisition of skills can be assured and experienced more extensively. Practice makes perfect. When I first came to China, every time I finished a ward round, I was left with a feeling of despondency, bemoaning the lack of an integrated and comprehensive range of medical services, unlike what was on offer back in the UK. I was not sure then of the competence level of our own staff either. These things take time and effort to fathom out. However, after eight years, every time I finish a ward round, I am left with a feeling of pride and some degree of satisfaction, of the competence of our medical staff, their willingness to learn the latest advances, and the comprehensive nature of our services. This certainly is not confined to my own specialty but spread right across all the specialties from surgical skills to procedural expertise.

I can now reveal some personal experience here. Some months ago, I had to undergo an invasive procedure known as cardiac catheterisation to assess my coronary arteries. This procedure involved using a very fine guide wire to be inserted precisely into the radial artery in the wrist. This guide wire was then threaded into the coronary arteries of the heart, to assess the adequacy of the blood supply to the heart by its own arteries. This was all done with local anaesthesia under radiological guidance. I chose to have this procedure performed in our own hospital because it was so much more convenient for me. If I were to have it done at Queen Mary Hospital in Hong Kong it would take up much more of my time. Because I chose to have this done as a public patient, I did not get to choose which cardiologist will be inserting the catheter for me, though I did have confidence in their practical skills. On the morning of the procedure, I was wheeled from the ward at 8.15 a.m. While I was lying under the X-ray machine, a gowned-up young doctor in a mask came to greet me and started the procedure, me having signed all the necessary consent forms the previous day. She was gentle, calm, and articulate. She verbally talked me through the whole procedure and in no time, she managed to insert the wire into my right radial artery and then a few minutes later I was able to see my own arterial flow into my heart on the X-ray screen! As it turned out, the result was good, and the arteries showed no further narrowing compared with the images done six years ago. I was relieved. The whole procedure took about 30 minutes, and I was back in the ward by 9.45 a.m. The point is, I did not know this doctor beforehand and it was an act of faith, based on my confidence in the skills and competency of our medical staff.

The best hospitals in China, spreading across major cities like Beijing, Shanghai, Guangzhou, Chengdu, or Hangzhou, can easily compete with the best in the US, the UK, or Europe in my view, in terms of the clinical competencies, the scope of their services and expertise. For every rare disease with an incidence of a few cases a year in the West, there may be three or four times more such diseases in China purely on epidemiological estimation, due to the large size of its population. The more you do, the better you become. Familiarity and experience breed expertise.

Another reason for this high level of competence may be the late presentation by the patients to seek medical attention, so the underlying condition may already be very advanced in nature. In addition, often their drug compliance can be poor and erratic in nature. I have seen a young patient who, after starting treatment for hypertension, felt better and decided that since he was feeling better, he stopped the tablet on his own accord without follow-up, only to turn up later with kidney failure. Or patients whose leukaemia is well controlled on chemotherapy, only to stop further treatment under no advice, unseen in the OPD, untraceable by phone, only to return later with a relapse of their leukaemia. Failure to attend follow-up clinics, even for some well-defined medical conditions, is common in China. Such habits, spread over a period of time over many patients, will lead to increased experience and competence for the doctors, in handling both the early stage of diseases and the late, advanced stages of disease, with its complications. This is regrettable. Acquiring enhanced expertise in dealing with late complications of diseases because of poor compliance of the patients clearly is a habit needed addressing by the collective and concerted effort of the medical community.

CHAPTER 21

Over-Investigations and Over-Prescriptions

Another often made comment on the medical services in China is the tendency to over-investigate with a wide range of diagnostic tests at our disposal. This can range from the use of the most basic and standard diagnostic and screening tools to the most esoteric ones such as genetics tests of unproven clinical value, and expensive imaging that few can afford. There is also a tendency to overprescribe too. These prescriptions can often be a combination of Western-based medicine plus numerous forms of health products such as vitamins. There are many reasons for these, and I can think of three main ones.

In modern Western medicine, diagnosis of a certain disease is based on the traditional model of detailed history taking, followed by a thorough physical examination, then backed up by supplementary diagnostic tests such as blood tests or X-ray. While the first two methods of diagnosis, primarily implemented by doctors, remain the same, the diagnostic tools these days have advanced to an almost unrecognisable form from my younger days. The imaging techniques are so sophisticated that radiology now has been divided into diagnostic radiology and interventional radiology. The latter means a procedure which can be carried out under X-ray monitor on a screen. This intervention can be for the purpose of obtaining a more accurate diagnosis such as the performance of a biopsy of a lesion in a specific organ or for the purpose of a specific life-saving procedure such as embolisation (creating a clot to block a bleeding blood vessel) for uncontrolled gastrointestinal bleeding. The reason it is done under X-ray screening on a monitor under aseptic condition is that it can enhance precision and safety.

The repertoire of blood tests can also be very wide-ranging, varying from testing on cells, the plasma, bacteria, or viral DNA to specific genetic mutations. These tests are very sophisticated to interpret. Their clinical significance can be very hard to assess for most doctors and often are very expensive to carry out too. They are so complicated that often an interpretational report is attached to the report to help the clinicians. Yet we strive to reach an accurate diagnosis without which we cannot formulate a treatment plan. So our tendency is to over investigate, especially in patients whose diagnosis may not be obvious from the beginning. By doing so, it is hoped that some tests will be positive in establishing a diagnosis. This is the 'spread the net wide and far, hoping something will be found' approach. In other words, hedging the bet by betting on everything!

The second reason is using tests to avoid complaints or litigations. It is very common for us to be questioned, or even challenged, by the patients and the families on why a certain test is not done. They base their knowledge on information obtained on the internet. Most Chinese these days are very smart in going onto the information superhighway. They are very seasoned netizens. They can check on the latest molecular tests identifying high risk acute leukaemia and ask if we have done it, even though such information may not have been fully validated in the professional community. Very often the validity of information obtained in this superhighway is not proven and yet it can be misused by some. Worse still if this is the subject of complaint where the diagnosis can be challenged. So the practice of over-investigation can reflect a tendency of a doctor to avoid complaints or litigation. This is regarded by us as moving away from practising cost-effective, evidence-based clinical medicine to the avoidance of disputes by practising defensive medicine.

The third reason, which may be more controversial but widely discussed nonetheless, is the extra tests, however clinically irrelevant or unnecessary they may be, may bring in more income, especially those tests not covered by state medical insurance. The tests covered by state insurance will be capped with a fixed price. The price of these extra and non-covered tests is often not regulated because they are not included in the state insurance. These tests are usually outsourced, often to a private company, and the price of these tests is often decided by the provider of services, while the consumers (the patients) have no say or choice. The doctors may act as an intermediary in requesting these tests. There is nothing wrong for us doctors acting as intermediaries, because it is our job to link up clinical conditions with diagnostic confirmation. It does, however, open up the possibility and indeed the impression that the more we do, the more we will generate income and the more it will help the hospital to have a balanced budget. At HKU SZH, our doctors, in requesting such outsourced tests will have to obtain signed consent from the patients before doing so and each will be recorded in the IT system for accountability and audit. If there is no signed consent for these tests, it is possible that the patients can default on payments, as these tests are often expensive.

The phenomenon of over-prescription can possibly be explained on the same basis. The more one prescribes, the more income is generated so often extremely cheap products, not even classified as medications, are prescribed, with a significant price mark up. This extra income will be a means of balancing the books for a hospital. One of the first things HKU SZH did was to regulate the prescription issue and stop the practice of over-prescription. Not only has HKU SZH policed overprescribing, there is no mark up for the price at all. In the OPD, the average number of items of prescription is just slightly over three in a medical specialty clinic. This practice has won very positive recognition by the Shenzhen government and beyond. It is now a government policy to prohibit the mark up of any drugs.

One other reason for over-prescription is possibly habitual. We Chinese do have a habit of thinking that, as far as medications are concerned, more is better. If someone goes to see a doctor for consultation and at the end of this the doctor reassures the patient that no treatment is necessary, it is entirely common for the patient to think he/she is not getting value-for-money for the consultation. After all, they have paid for the appointment fee upfront already so why no medications afterwards! They may not accept that the principle here is to seek a medical opinion which may or may not lead to the prescription of medications. A common example is in the case of a flu-like illness, most people do know about the needs for rest and hydration in this condition, perhaps adding some mild analgesics for headache and muscle pain. These can be obtained over the counter in any pharmacy. Some patients however still wish to see a doctor for prescriptions, often even asking to be given intravenous infusion at the same time. The other common example is an overweight middle age, otherwise healthy man, was found to have mild hypertension which clearly the treatment of first choice is weight loss. Again, this may be unacceptable to the patient who may not wish to change his lifestyle so opting instead for the easier option of taking tablets.

The above tendencies can be changed. It takes time and involves public education in all its forms. It is very gratifying to note, certainly in Shenzhen, that there are many TV or radio programmes promoting public health with emphasis on how lifestyle changes can improve health. There are many public video clips on this on the internet. These video clips are very simple to understand and produced for the purpose of public education so there are no commercial promotional purposes in them. Our own hospital also regularly organises education forums for the public, both in our own premises and outside such as civic halls.

CHAPTER 22

Choice, Flexibility, and Competition

Since the launch of the market-based economy in China in the early 1980s, the provision of hospital services has by and large adopted a similar model, where 'Money Follows the Patient' is the key principle for both public and private hospitals. The key aim of this principle is that patients can have a choice on where they seek medical services, be it the primary care in the community or specialist in the hospital. In the UK, this Money Follows the Patient concept has been a constant area for debates over many decades. The NHS is now more than 70 years old. In the UK, everyone is assigned a primary care doctor (General Practitioner, known as GP) in the local area and any referral to a specialist can only be initiated by the primary care doctor, thus serving a gatekeeping role. Therefore, the patients nearly always have to follow the advice of the GPs, especially who and where they are referred to see the specialists. Ideologically, this is seen as lack of choice by the consumers, and in the case of the NHS, lack of choice by the patients. The advocates for such a Money Follows the Patient model argue that this limitation of choice and flexibility for the patients is inconsistent with the modern economic theory of a free market system in which the market knows best on how to allocate resources, through choices and competition, to meet the rising demands. This fundamental principle, so they argue, can and should apply to medical services too.

The UK Experience

In the UK, each attempt over the past decades has failed to deliver this market-based model, partly because the NHS, being a taxation-funded service, is seen by the electorate as a beloved beacon, a fair system for all and a noble concept. This much-loved NHS is felt to be owned by and provided for the people via taxation. The principles of the UK NHS, established 70 years ago, are: Free at the Point of Delivery, Cradle to Grave approach from birth to death are cherished by all in the UK despite the uncontrollable rising costs of healthcare. In other words, all British citizens from birth to death are entitled to free medical care regardless of the ability to pay. These are the main ideological reasons put forward by those who are antagonistic to the Money Follows the Patient Principle. And yet, the funding principle established 70 years ago is constantly met with financial stress in view of the uncontrolled cost inflation of medical advances and the ageing population. To fund such a resource-draining service via general taxation means that inevitably it would be at the expense of other public services. The free marketeers see the NHS as a monopoly, and the discipline inherent in a market economy and capitalist society where productivity and competition are the key engines for growth are lacking in such a monopoly and are not subject to any market discipline. This is the predominant view held by the pro-market supporters who point out that the system in the UK is an outdated socialist system where the funding is state directed, inconsistent with the economic system in a capitalist country.

What actually happens in the UK is that the funding goes directly to the various providers of services such as hospitals, ambulance services, community healthcare centres, and primary care doctors (General Practitioners, or GPs). There are some individual payments which need to be paid for by the patients such as the use of hospital beds or items of prescription but even these payments can be exempted for the poor. The main disadvantage, so the critics of this system point out, is that as a result, there is a cartel consisting of all stakeholders of various providers, which monopolises how the services are run, and the staff working in the system are protected from the discipline of competition and the need for improved productivity. Such a cartel has an inherent resistance to change that may threaten the status quo. As such, the patients often do not have a choice or say in where they want to go and who they want to see. In short, choice by the patients and competition for services are stifled, leading to stagnation, inertia, and waste of resources. The providers of services decide what to do while the users of services have little say. They also argue, with some justification, that in the face of medical costs potentially spiralling out of control, some sort of market-based reforms will help to control cost and improve productivity by competition.

The China Practice

In China, there is a real demonstration of Money Follows the Patient principle. I was initially not very accustomed to this as I had previously worked in and got used to the UK system. But I soon realised that Money Follows the Patient does have its advantages.

First, the patients here are often regarded as 'customers' to be served, even if they may, by definition, have some ailments, a concept not dissimilar to a customer going for dinner in a restaurant. The service providers, i.e. the hospitals, know that these patients always have a choice and their choice of which hospital to seek such services from will often depend on how famous the hospital is (those in Beijing and Shanghai always come at the top, while there are other famous hospitals from all over China too), how credible the hospital is, and of course how easy it is to get an appointment. Often the patients base their decision by checking with friends and the internet as well, since China boasts the smartest netizens I have ever known! For those who have state medical insurance, such as those working and residing in a major front-line city like Shenzhen, they can choose where to go for consultation and who to see, then pay upfront and reclaim a significant portion from the local government, much like an insurance company. This is true Money Follows the Patient at work. The patient or their families decide where to go without the need for any specialist referral. Being smart netizens, most of them will know which specialty to choose anyway, such as for cough and fever, they would choose to attend a respiratory unit. For those who are not sure which specialty to go for, they can choose to attend the six-day/week GP clinic at HKU SZH.

This flexibility is in sharp contrast to that in the UK where seeking specialist opinions is always dependent on the gatekeeping process of referrals by the GP. No one can go to a hospital to see a specialist without a GP referral. The only exception is if the patient is willing to pay for a private consultation which, in the UK, is not a mainstream service (less than 10% of attendances are private patients and are mostly in London). Even if a referral is made by a GP, the hospital of choice is often based on its geographical location and proximity, not on the basis of the reputation of the hospital. A request made by a patient in Liverpool to seek specialty referral in Manchester will not be granted by the GP, unless that specialty is not available in Liverpool. In China, the referral system can include self-referral, and there is no gate keeping. The advantage of the China model is that it entirely depends on the patient's wish and in exercising that wish, patients can be very flexible in deciding where and when they wish to go, and even if they cannot make a scheduled appointment for personal reasons, the appointment can be rescheduled within a matter of days, not weeks or even months, as in the UK. So choice and flexibility go hand in hand, a demonstrable example of Money Follows the Patient model, with convenience and efficiency as added value from the patients' point of view. Waiting time is a constant problem in the UK while it is non-existent in China.

However, this model does have its disadvantages and critics. Because of the flexibility described above, patients are likely to misuse this flexibility, leading to a strange phenomenon of 'doctor shopping'. That is, patients can often choose to see doctors from one hospital to another for a second, third, or sometimes even fourth opinion. It probably reflects a lack of confidence or trust in the doctors. The reasons for this may be very complex but it can undoubtedly lead to waste of precious resources, especially in diagnostics. Often the same test can be repeatedly requested for really no additional clinical benefits. Patients here choose where and when to go, not on the advice of a relatively professional well-informed and impartial advisor such as a GP but rather through their own perceived ideas based on reputation of the hospitals and recommendations by friends.

Competition Among Hospitals

The other main area for contention is that as a result of this Money Follows the Patient system, there is always competition between hospitals. The motto is that those who see the highest number of patients, who carry out the most surgeries, who prescribe most drugs, and who request most diagnostics tests will bring in the most income, thus making the hospital not only financially secure but even profitable. In the mindset of the people, a busy and profitable hospital must mean that this hospital is good. How else can it be successful? So, hospitals compete on the number of attendances, the number of operations performed, and the range of services provided. There is nothing wrong with the principle of competition and in fact, economists always uphold the notion that competition is the key to economic prosperity and progress since everyone in this game will seek to improve by enhancing productivity. In the medical field, the hospitals in China will always compete with each other, striving to seek clinical excellence, to achieve national reputation, to have the highest number of patients, and to be in a higher position in the ranking. No one ever wants to be the loser and be at the bottom, everyone wants to be successful and be at the top of the game.

The question here is, how would one define competition in the medical field, how can one ensure benign and constructive competition among a group of hospitals, and in so doing, how do we ensure probity and governance in all this? Probity, safety, and governance are all inbuilt requirements in the day-to-day operation of a good and safe hospital. Will these be compromised in the face of competition? On the other hand, the staff all need to make a living, and they need bonuses to make up for the basically low salaries, so they would almost always accept that the hospital they work in not only has to be competitive, but compete to be more successful, since success will bring in revenue. Because of the lack of gatekeeping role by the GP, unlike in the UK, who acts as a professional third party, this competition is potentially likely to be intense and becomes unchecked. There is no clear answer to this very fundamental question of the role of competition in the medical field. It will need political scientists and health economists to come up with a view, if ever a view is possible. A profitable hospital may not necessarily be a good hospital while a good hospital will be profitable in the long run.

My own view on this complicated question, after eight years of working in a major hospital in China, is that I would venture to state that, by and large, competition for services in China is positive and constructive. The advantage is to the patients, not to the doctors as the incentive will always be in improving the clinical services to attract more work. If a patient will need a two-week wait for elective surgery for a non-life-threatening condition, while another hospital can provide the same service within a week, then the beneficiary will be the patient. Eight years working in China has convinced me Money Follows the Patient is the preferred model since it places patients at the centre of the service and top of its priority list. Healthy competition for patients among peers would enhance both service quality and efficiency.

Hospital Rankings

There are many ways a hospital can compete and promote its reputation. The first one is of course national ranking. In China, just like the USA, there is an annual ranking of all the hospitals in terms of their clinical expertise, the sort of top ten hospitals list. How exactly the ranking is done I am not too sure, but it is not the mechanism of the ranking that matters in the minds of the patients, but the position in the ranking list that matters. To be ranked high takes years to achieve, as a solid reputation will depend on the consistency in excellence of services, in research, and in publication. All these will take years to plan and develop, not to mention good teamwork. In the ranking exercise, just like university ranking, it has been the same group of hospitals that come up top every year, based on their long and distinguished services. No hospital I know of with a short history ever comes up even in the top 50. Good and safe medical services should be self-evident given in any hospital. The tight accreditation process I described in Chapter 11 should be a good safety net. In my own experience, it was indeed not infrequent when I first started eight years ago that patients diagnosed with a blood cancer asked to be discharged (not referred or transferred) so they could choose to go to a top-ranking hospital in Guangzhou or Beijing for treatment. It was because I was new to the scene and hence did not have a locally established reputation. Patients with a life-threatening illness such as leukaemia were understandably concerned about the set-up in a brand-new hospital for such a complicated disease. However, these requests for discharges have become much less common in the last few years. The point I am trying to make here is that clinical credibility cannot be established overnight. In fact, it is wrong and dangerous to do so.

There are other ways to compete for reputation other than ranking, research, or publications, such as piloting cutting-edge and innovative techniques or procedures to attract more patients or participating in a major multicentre clinical trial with other major premier hospitals, or encouraging senior specialists taking a leading national role in being an executive member of a national committee. These are all very acceptable and common ways to ensure reputation and the prestige of a hospital. Thus, patients will naturally and willingly be attracted to seek attention in hospitals which have many consultants or professors of national reputation.

Another way of competing, which I think is unique in China, is to use easily understandable data to promote popularity and desirability among the public. The marker for these may be its OPD attendance numbers, monthly or yearly. One key data that health care planning managers always look at in a hospital is its annual OPD figures, which not only can help to predict its financial but also its competitive position among its peers. High numbers of OPD means not only high demands, but also demonstrates popularity. A restaurant which is always so full of diners must mean the food is good. A hospital is no different.

Competitiveness and reputation of a hospital can also be improved through the work of the Public Relations Department, which is present in every hospital. Good human stories are spread and shared with the public, conditional on the consent of the patients. There is a close collaboration between the Public Relations Department with the various platforms in the media, such as press, radio, television, and even social media, in sharing out new services and achievements. One of the ways which needs special mention is that some hospitals, HKU SZH included, actually host public education events to promote public health, often in the evenings or weekends, in civic halls, or libraries, on a non-paid and voluntary basis. Our medical and nursing staff volunteer to give public healthcare-related lectures with open questions and answers sessions. I see this as a very commendable effort in using one's own professional knowledge to help others for free. I have taken part in these events on a regular basis myself and have enjoyed them, as I can tell these are well accepted by the public with enthusiasm. At HKU SZH, patient forums for each specialty are held regularly too in the main atrium, with education lectures given, stories by patients shared, and little souvenirs handed out. In fact, when HKU SZH was awarded the ACHS accreditation, one of the marks of distinction that was highlighted by ACHS was the hospital's effort in public education events.

Choice for Self-Financing Patients

One area worthy of special mention in the discussion of patients' choice is that at HKU SZH, there is a private wing called the International Medical Centre (IMC) serving private patients who choose personally to see a named consultant or professor at HKU SZH. This IMC provides both inpatient and outpatient facilities. The service is entirely fee paying either by personal means or by commercial health insurance scheme but not government or state insurance. The aim of this IMC is to offer those patients who are willing to pay extra for a designated service from a named consultant or professor, while extra income can be generated for this hospital. The income generated does not lead to increased personal income for any individual but will be regarded as hospital income with part of it awarded to departments on a pro rata basis. The clinical service is no different from the non-private patients, though the ambience may be more comfortable as the IMC is in a separate block with single rooms or suites. The perfect analogy is like travelling long distance on a Boeing 747 from Beijing to London, both the business class and economy class will be carrying the same passengers safely from A to B, though the business class passengers pay more for more comfortable service, while the flight attendants get equal salary. In medical care, the rich deserve us no less than the poor or vice versa.

CHAPTER 23

Undergraduate and Postgraduate Specialty Training

This Chapter is focused to shed some light on why in recent years the clinical competence of the medical profession in China has reached a higher level of standards. Throughout the whole of China, there has been real progress in standardising undergraduate training for the profession since the early 1980s when reforms in many areas were a national priority, education being one of them. Years ago, medical undergraduate training varied hugely from university to university, from region to region, and even the years required for training and internship can be different. The model of undergraduate training, the curriculum, the teaching requirements, and examinations are now much more standardised and structured. The contents of the curriculum are not only up to date, but the methods of teaching can take various forms, incorporating various modern methods of teaching using multimedia, small group discussion, and self-initiated studies. Both teachers and students are regularly assessed. This, in my view, is the main reason for the improvement of standards.

The postgraduate training, however, can still be a bit fragmented and unstructured. The standard career pathway is still much the same from the time of graduation. It starts as interns, then to residents in specialties as part of a rotation programme to gain more clinical experience in various specialties, and then enter into a chosen specialty. A national senior examination then follows and once passed, one can theoretically apply for a more senior post (equivalent to a consultant post in the UK) in open competition. In practice, it does not always work that way. In the UK and in Hong Kong, the postgraduate training for any chosen specialty is structured. However, in China, there is no standard professional guidance or advice given to the young trainees, especially in the assessment and the choice between an academic career and a clinical career for a given trainee. So, these graduates are often encouraged to do both academic research work leading to the award of a Master Degree or PhD, while simultaneously continuing to perform very heavy clinical duties as residents. This may not be a problem in the past when life as a doctor was not that demanding. However, in these days of specialisation and sub-specialisation, this approach arguably may not be suitable for every young doctor and even inappropriate for us to expect them to do both clinical work, for which they are paid, and research work, for which they are not paid, or paid very minimally.

Within the medical profession, some young doctors may be truly interested in research and academic work while others may excel at clinical work. Doing proper research requires one to be properly supervised and focused, with a single mindedness of purpose, protected from distraction by day-to-day clinical demands. For those wishing to do both research, especially with a view to publishing papers, and clinical work, it is invariable that most of their time is spent on clinical work in the wards due to hospital demands, as the hospital is the pay master while their research time is not protected. Thus, their time to carry out meaningful research or clinical studies will be very limited, necessitating most of them to spend their own time on their research, which is unsustainable in the long term. Often too, the aspirations to work for a Master or PhD can be misplaced, using the achievements of such work not as a means of intellectual enrichment but more so as a means of seeking publications and thus career promotion.

The emphasis on research and publications is due to the fact that most major hospitals in China will insist on publications and higher degrees such as Master/PhD as one of the benchmarks for promotion. It means that if one wishes to reach a high position in one's career, one needs to have not only good specialist medical training, but also needs research work and publications in trying to reach the top. Not everyone, however, is endowed with all these three talents. Those without these perfect three will be disfranchised, ending up feeling frustrated or discontented. I have enough personal experience in all these years to draw the conclusion that some doctors carry out their clinical work to an extremely high standard but for them, their promotion prospects are restrained due to lack of publications. These doctors would, in my own judgement, have no problems being promoted to be a consultant in the UK. This system in China to me therefore is perhaps too rigid. It is common for a hospital to boast how many PhD supervisors and PhD holders they have. In my opinion, a good hospital should strive to have a balanced mix of good, skilled doctors without PhDs as well as those with PhDs and thesis supervisors, the latter focusing on research or clinical trials leading to publications. In serving the public and striving for academic distinctions, a hospital needs both sets of skills. Academic brilliance may not equate clinical brilliance and vice versa. Too rigid an approach may lead to dishonesty or even plagiarism, not to mention undue stress, and misguided aspirations for these doctors.

The UK Training Model

Similar problems were faced in the UK many years ago but then a new programme of structured postgraduate training was launched in which there is now a twin-track approach. In the postgraduate system in the UK, there is now a specific academic track for an academic career and a service track for a clinical career. Compared with the past in the UK, the overall time required for each track is shortened by two to three years, so early talents in both tracks can be spotted and the age of reaching a consultant or professor can be younger. In addition, there is now also the established notion that reaching the level of consultant is just the start of a career and will require post consultant assessment and education. The UK General Medical Council (GMC), the institution responsible for issuing medical licence to practice, has started a process called revalidation in which all consultants have to go through every five years. I myself was among the first batch of consultants that have gone through this revalidation when I was last working in the UK. It was very comprehensive and detailed, the emphasis is on a descriptive reflection on my work, my interaction with colleagues, and what effort I had made in seeking continued personal developments. Publications are desirable but not mandatory. This is the UK GMC's efforts to safeguard standards, and to ensure continued medical education and professionalism.

In China, one key area where there is an urgent need for development in both the undergraduate and postgraduate training is primary care. China is a big country with many ethnic minorities in areas with different cultures, habits, and climatic conditions, so lifestyle and disease patterns can vary from region to region. Appreciation of this will be a key to the development of a good primary care, enabling medical services to be tailored to fit better with the local needs. In addition, many diseases are lifestyle diseases, often amenable to relatively straightforward treatment. These lifestyle diseases such as hypertension, diabetes, coronary heart diseases, kidney impairment, not only are common but are also easily diagnosable or detectable by early, affordable, and effective screening. Early treatment of such chronic and common diseases can actually prevent later complications. And since these conditions are common, it will be more cost effective if the primary care sector can be the core provider group caring for these patients. This will free up the always overloaded hospitals to provide care for the more complicated cases. Setting up such primary care centres staffed by well-trained doctors can be more cost effective and less dependent on expensive tests. The 'barefoot doctors' concept in the 1960s can now be replaced by well-trained primary doctors work force to treat the common conditions of the masses and patients in villages do not have to attend the big hospital in the metropolis.

The concept of 'barefoot doctors' needs further explanations in the context of the history of modern health care in China. In the 1960s, China was poor, suffering then from the failed social movement called The Great Leap Forward. Malnutrition was common and hygiene standards were poor, especially in the villages. So, Chairman Mao, faced with the urgent need to resolve this widespread problem, sent out what he called barefoot doctors to go to the villages to distribute vitamins, antiseptics to wounds, and educate the peasants on basic healthcare. These were not properly trained doctors in the Western sense but were fast tracked to become healthcare professionals to serve the national need. This initiative in my view should not be sneered at. It served the need as at that time the most urgent healthcare need was the basic improvement of personal hygiene, the correction of malnutrition and vitamins deficiency.

The importance of primary care provision is now fully recognised and accepted by the central government. It is now the stated policy of the government in setting up a structured training program for General Practice (GP) as a specific specialty. This is to be welcomed. In fact, HKU SZH is the first hospital which has set up a General Practice (GP) Department since 2012, led and run by the Academic Department of General Practice of the Medical Faculty in HKU. Such a set-up was so innovative that various experts and health officials have often come to visit the department regularly over the years. Extensive discussions with senior health officials in Guangdong province then followed. As a result, the General Practice Department was the first department in Shenzhen to receive official approval with a licence issued as a training centre for General Practice by the provincial government of Guangdong, a province which boasts a population of 110 million people. Newly qualified doctors who wish to specialise in General Practice are assigned to HKU SZH for a certifiable training period of three years with an updated core curriculum designed by the Department of General Practice. Over the last few years, I have already met and taught many of these trainees with much personal enthusiasm, knowing they will be a key part of a very modern primary care system for China.

I mentioned before the high clinical standards in the major hospitals in China, so how else can they maintain this standard? Apart from the tried and tested formula of attendance at professional meetings, checking the journals and textbooks for the latest advances and treatments, group discussion and presentation on cases, what else is there to enhance learning and information sharing?

Just like the Medscape in the USA and the Doctors.net in the UK,

China also has a similar internet-based institution for netizens. It is called Ding Xiang Yuan (DXY.cn), a short for lilac garden in Chinese. It is a leading connector and digital service provider for the healthcare industry in China. Founded 19 years ago, it is now the leading online forum for doctors from all specialties, offering a whole range of services, such as professional information, e-education, connecting doctors, researchers, pharmacists, with a registration containing 5.5 million life science members, including two million doctors. It provides information for the professionals, the public, the academic institutions, and commercial organisations such as the pharmaceuticals. I joined DXY.cn in 2018 and have found the scope of its services and the content of its information truly impressive. No wonder my medical colleagues are frequently talking about it and recommended me to join, offering me another avenue for learning, even when I am in the UK!

CHAPTER 24

Medical Research

Western medical research methodology and its emphasis on science are based on basic studies of physiology, biochemistry, anatomy, and pharmacology, using data, scientific findings, and statistics. In the past, scientific contributions and the studies during the long history of Traditional Chinese Medicine (TCM) in China, though very well recorded and thoroughly described, were not scientifically documented or validated. This is because TMC is not regarded as based on science, as the way science is regarded in the West. The essence of TCM has already been described briefly in Chapter 15. Broadly speaking, many of the main and famous, ground-breaking discoveries in China throughout its history were made out of observations and practical considerations. The most famous ones were the magnet for navigation, the gunpowder for fireworks, the making of paper for writing, and the art of printing for replications and record keeping. Basic approach to science in the Western world using as its tools for the studies of biology, chemistry, mathematics, and physics was never the main approach used by the Chinese scholars. In fact, I am not sure if the word 'scientist' ever has a suitable translation in China in the past, which, in its long civilisation, was mainly focused on the importance of literacy, peasantry, craftsmanship, and commerce.

Regrettably also, many great inventions of significance in China were not widely practised or actively introduced to the outside world.

For instance, we might have invented gunpowder for fireworks display for various festivals as celebrations and yet the full potential of such an invention, both for industrial and military purposes, was developed by the West. The invention of the abacus is another example. This invention was ground-breaking, simple, and elegant. It uses rows and columns of movable balls and sticks, made of wood, along an axis to make quick calculations. I used to play with it as a child and was utterly amazed how clever it was. But even something as widely practised as the abacus in China is now replaced by calculators which emerged after the Second Industrial Revolution, which China failed to capitalise on. The use of the abacus in China is now near extinct. This is known by economists as creative destruction. It means that the successful development of a new product based on new technology for the consumers at an affordable price will reach such popularity that it will replace the traditional product. Kodak was ubiquitous once but now no longer exists as none of us use films for photos anymore. The famous, once global blockbuster Sony Walkman in the early 1980s met a similar fate. People use digital music and streaming but not tapes or CDs anymore. So scientific advances and their applications are a never-ending process. Science and research must be both creative and sustainable.

The way I see it, the Western approach is through observation and deduction (the Theory of Evolution), scientific measurements and calculations (the molecular weight of water and its chemical formula), and thought experiment, worked out by mathematics and proved by real life experiments ($E=MC^2$). The Chinese way of approach to science is more philosophical and metaphysical, by observing cosmology and the earth, by thinking of the balance of interactions, sun and moon, heat and cold, yin and yang, etc and often such an approach will make validation and confirmation by experimental data very difficult if not impossible.

All the classic textbooks in medicine in Chinese history were based on observations (such as the state of the tongue), crude measurements (feeling the pulse), the concept of yin (negativity) and yang (positivity). These of course have deep philosophical meaning and their acceptance by the Chinese is not without reason since it is based on thousands of years of experience, even in the absence of scientific evidence. The same approach is adopted in the use of herbal or animal extracts to cure diseases. Indeed, this does sometimes work. For instance, the common advice for some Chinese is that eating liver (very rich in iron and iron deficiency anaemia is indeed very common) is good for anyone with anaemia but in the West, one has to know the cause of this anaemia, which can be anything other than iron deficiency, in which case eating liver does not work. This is the different Western approach, which is based on physiology, biochemistry, or anatomical science. It is difficult to be precise when Western medicine was first introduced in China. Some would guess it was around the 16th century through the arrival of the Jesuit missionaries, who first arrived at Macao, a Portuguese colony in the southern part of China. But this Western medicine by and large had little impact then. It was only after the arrival of more missionaries in the late 19th and early 20th centuries that Western medicine was introduced on a wider scale. Not only did these missionaries introduce Western medicine, they actually practised it too, as most of them had medical or nursing training. So, Western medicine, to be fair, has a very short history in China, perhaps no more than 200 years.

As a result, medical research based on the Western approach in the new and modern China started quite late, and China has a lot of catching up to do. With the gradual rise of China in the modern world, the central government quickly realised that the country needs to make progress and strides in scientific advance, research, and its know-how. The aim is to change China from an agricultural nation to a modern industrialised nation. This change was actively supported by the Chinese people. Every educational and research institution now emphasises the importance of STEM (science, technology, engineering, and mathematics). Universities now offering courses in these subjects are very popular and competition for places from national entry examinations is intense. This process of catching up started 40 years ago, at the start of the reforms, China has since made huge strides in these four areas, and in some specific scientific areas, such as the biosciences, are regarded as one of the world leaders. The main reason for this success in China is the significant investment in the resources made available by the central government in the awards of state-funded research grants, especially in recent years. In 2017, China spent an equivalent of USD279 billion on research and development, a staggering increase of 14% compared to the previous year. In total, China spent 2.1% of its GDP on research while the USA spent 2.8% of its GDP on research. It is likely that China will overtake the USA in the next decade in this regard. Funding of course does not guarantee success, but it is nonetheless indispensable. It is a primer in attracting the best talents and buying cutting-edge equipment. The research fund is often granted as a programme, which can be tens of millions of RMB, with a very tight peer review process to such grant applications and even a tighter process to monitor progress.

Progress in China's Medical Research

In my early years as a doctor in the UK, there were hardly any publications in scientific journals with Chinese-named authors. Then gradually things started to change, very slowly but surely, from the early eighties. I began to notice some Chinese names appearing in such journals, often part of a team in a well-known academic or research institution in the West, especially the USA. Most of the Chinese participants in these papers were scientists from China doing important laboratory-based research abroad, possibly through government or institutional sponsorships for a certain period of time. At the same time, the Chinese government also started to support and invest heavily in the home-grown scientific research community in mainland Chinese institutions. It also encourages collaboration with international institutions as part of a wider scientific exchange and in so doing, to learn and adopt the Western vigilance and methodology in doing scientific research. There are now early and encouraging signs that this process is beginning to bear fruit.

One noticeable result in the medical field is that there are now more clinical scientific papers published solely on work done in China. Clinical scientific papers mean that the area for research is directly relevant to the day-to-day practice of medicine. This may include new diagnostic tests and new treatments, using new scientific advances in molecular biology or genomics as a foundation to understand the cellular, molecular, or genetic basis of diseases and its pathogenesis. This is, in the medical profession, called translational research and that means the basic research has progressed or matured to a stage where it becomes possible to be applied in clinical practice. Just the other day, my colleagues told me, with great pride, that three clinical papers on work done in China were simultaneously published in the same issue from the highly prestigious *New England Journal of Medicine*. Publishing one paper in that journal from one institution is a lifelong ambition, publishing three in the same issue of work from the same institution is truly impressive and rare. Moreover, these are clinical publications on the world's first ever clinical trial using a new oral medication to improve the haemoglobin (correction of anaemia) levels in Chinese patients with kidney failure. In the past, such clinical trials and results could only be coming from research work carried out in the West. These successes indicate that the pharmacological giants are now willing to consider China as a primary centre or a key centre for any new potential ground-breaking clinical research. China and its research community are demonstrably quickly catching up. The huge patient database is also a significant contributing factor. While it may take other countries to amass significant numbers of patients in testing for advances over a long period of time, China can do this in a much shorter time frame as the population is so big.

Just like many other areas in our pursuit of excellence, there will be needs for caution in achieving success. On matters of clinical research, vigilance, probity, and validation are the key ingredients of research governance. Data, results, and conclusions must be subjected to the closest scrutiny by the scientific community. In the past, submitted scientific papers often had the validity of the data questioned, detailed technological know-how was doubted, and even falsified data was unearthed, reflecting an underlying need for scientific integrity and probity. Occasionally the papers published had to be withdrawn from the journals, thus darkening the reputation and the credibility of the teams and institutions in China.

Can we justifiably view this as a growing pain of a maturing research mentality in China? I think we can. The majority of recent publications are now fully validated. The three key core principles of ethics, scientific integrity, and validity of original data in any research work are being implemented and compliance is expected of all in the scientific community. A report in 2019 by *Lancet* (Asia office), one of the top medical journals in the world, stated that over the last 10 years, the *Lancet* has seen Chinese papers surge from a few hundred to some 1,500 annually, ranking third globally after the UK and the USA. More and more scholars and researchers from China are being invited to speak in major scientific conferences around the world. I know that new cutting-edge medical research is already happening and taking root in some top academic institutions in China. These areas include studying the genetic basis of diseases, personally genetic based precision medicine, new anticancer therapy based on immunity or on altering the normal molecular pathways to modify the cellular behaviours to stop cancer cells from growing or even the most precise of targeted therapy using nanotechnology. Other important areas China is heavily investing in are infection control and public health. Advances in these areas are around the corner in the next five to 10 years. Many institutions in China are already working intensely on these and some of these products are already undergoing clinical testing and a few of them will soon be on the horizon of being launched. In this respect, China is undoubtedly heading in the right direction. It is almost certain that China, based on its huge and sustained efforts in undertaking modern scientific research, will be a key stakeholder, playing a leading role in such advances.

PART 3: COVID-19

CHAPTER 25

From Endemic to Pandemic

This chapter was conceived and written in late March 2020. The world was then gripped with fear and anxiety by the COVID-19 viral outbreak. It started barely four months ago in December 2019 with the first cases from Wuhan in China and, within this short period, barely a country in the world was unaffected, except the uninhibited continents; the Arctic and the Antarctica. The scale, the speed, and the intensity were unprecedented in the 21st century and the fear that was generated was compared with the Spanish Flu in 1918 and SARS (Severe Acute Respiratory Syndrome) in 2003. The Spanish Flu lasted two years while SARS lasted about six months. I think it is too mature, as some commentators do, to raise comparison with the Spanish Flu. The general nutritional status of the modern-day population is better, living and hygiene standards are better, and preventative measures are more effective. It will be a gross failure on our part if this current pandemic is allowed to be developed into anything remotely close to the Spanish Flu. Nevertheless, the COVID-19 crisis was global within just four months, spreading like wildfire. Nearly all countries, without exception, were caught unprepared, even though some countries might be initially aware of the spread of this outbreak following the global alert from the World Health Organisation (WHO).

While some is known about the virus grouped as belonging to the Coronavirus families, and thus bears some resemblance to SARS in Asia in 2003 and MERS (Middle East Respiratory Syndrome) in 2012, more is unknown about this virus than is known. The mortality is so tragically high, especially among those who had ongoing health conditions, the elderly, and male. People, both the professionals and the public, unknowingly and understandably, thought initially that this might be a case of severe seasonal flu, but this view was quickly disapproved by the rapidly transforming and alarming scenes from all over the world. WHO declared this as a pandemic. No health service system in the world can cope with this sudden onslaught. Each country has to make rapid adjustments and re-arrangements in its health services in dealing with this crisis. Some of these adjustments are dramatic and ground-breaking.

Global economy was under threat. The last global financial crisis in 2008, which was caused by reckless lending, initiated in Wall Street in the USA and then copied by the rest of the world in the pursuit of profit at the expense of the innocents and the uninformed, was primarily greed in nature. In other words, greed created and perpetuated by humans. This time, the global economy is threatened in an unimaginable scale because the virus does not differentiate between US Dollars, Chinese RMB, Euros, or gold bars, national boundaries or cultures. It attacks and affects wherever it goes, every human being, rich and poor, young and old. So the threat is clear, immediate, and potentially apocalyptic for humanities.

The word war is appropriately used by many, though this is a war fought by humans against a tiny piece of RNA. This war is a global effort to fight against the virus, using all tools available to help the suffering and its impact on the non-suffering. In general, in medicine at least, prevention is always better than cure. But in this case, at the time of writing, prevention from the outbreak was no longer possible. It has by March become a pandemic. All that was commonly agreed by nearly all epidemiologists was that the best we can hope for is to press the population infection curve down. In other words, containment was no longer possible, and we have to turn to mitigation. So, the tools at our disposals would vary from public health education, advice, recommendation, legislation, experimental treatments, clinical trials, and the holy grail of all prevention against transmissible diseases, the vaccine. All these need to be done, none can guarantee success but together the benefits can be significant and effective. Governments, health agencies, and the public seem to put much hope on the quick availability of a vaccine, I also sincerely hope so too, but it would be careless of me if I do not point out that right now, the last outbreaks that caused such fear were the HIV and SARS, neither has led to a vaccine, though the former is now treatable. Whether a COVID-19 vaccine will be made available like the flu vaccine or not is too early to say, and it takes time to validate its efficacy. Hopes may run high, but reality checks are needed. For other major diseases like malaria, vaccines are still some way off. During this period therefore, it is better to be honest with the public than raising their expectations, as the public is generally already very scared.

One of the tools in public health education is on how to reduce or even prevent the infection of a given individual. With all the facets of this health education and protection of individuals, a whole new set of vocabularies has emerged. This includes social distancing, self-isolation, a distance of about two metres from each other, no mass gathering, work from home, online meetings via Zoom, clinical phone consultation, lockdowns, hand washings, wiping down all hard surfaces with antiseptics, epidemiological modelling, personal protective equipment (PPE), herd immunity, tests, contact tracing, and the widespread use of masks, which will be an area for further detailed discussion here.

It is the question of using masks which is most controversial, not only between nations but mainly between the East and the West, between the scientists and the epidemiologists. As a doctor working in HKU SZH at the height of the crisis in China from early February to mid-March 2020, and then, going back to my families in the UK, I see a stark contrast in attitude, almost a 180 degree contrast, in the use of mask between the East and the West. It is this contrast that sets me up on the idea of this additional section, worthy of further discussion in this book. Through this discussion, I would explore if a consensus for an accepted practice can be reached and if so, how can this be achieved.

For the purpose of understanding the scale of the global crisis and how astonishingly quick this virus spread globally, a brief description and chronology of the key events is needed.

Chronology of Events

This outbreak started in Wuhan in December 2019. Wuhan is a major city in China with a population of 11 million and is a major transportation hub for China. The importance of this hub is best illustrated by data showing that on January 1st 2020, 750,000 people left Wuhan on a single day and in the first three weeks of January, before the Spring Festival, it is estimated that about 7 million people had left Wuhan.

December 31st 2019, the World Health Organisation was notified of the outbreak of atypical viral pneumonia by China.

January 3rd 2020, Chinese scientists at the National Institute for Viral Disease Control and Prevention (IVDC) determined successfully the genetic sequence of the novel β-genus coronaviruses (naming it '2019-nCoV').

January 10th, first two patients in Shenzhen attended the HKU SZH, where I work. The two patients were then transferred into negative pressure rooms in Third People's Hospital of Shenzhen City (the infectious disease hospital in Shenzhen) due to matching lab test result, symptoms, and epidemiology and were listed as suspected cases.

January 13th, Thailand witnessed the first confirmed case of 2019-nCoV, the first outside China.

January 20th, Chinese premier Li Keqiang urged decisive and effective efforts to prevent and control the epidemic.

January 23rd, Wuhan was locked down.

The Spring Festival (also known as Lunar New Year based on the Chinese lunar calendar) started on January 25th for a seven-day long national holiday break. For this festival, it is also a standard practice in China that all factories will be closed for a period of two weeks, to enable the workers to be reunited with their families at their hometowns.

January 30th, WHO declared Public Health Emergency of International Concern.

February 11th, WHO named novel coronavirus disease COVID-19.

February 25th, WHO-China Joint Mission set up to share findings and recommendations.

March 3rd, WHO announced global shortages of personal protective equipment for health care workers.

March 7th, Global cases reached 100,000.

March 11th, WHO declared COVID-19 as pandemic.

March 13th, Europe surpassed China in reported cases and became the epicentre of the pandemic.

March 27th, global total of cases passed 500,000.

April 3rd, global cases passed 1,000,000 (70,000 deaths) and the figures kept growing.

April 30th, global cases passed 3,000,000 (217,000 deaths) and the USA alone had more than 1,000,000 cases (57,000 deaths).

So, in a short span of four months, COVID-19 has affected more than 3,000,000 and claimed the lives of more than 217,000 people all over the world. The numbers far exceeded those of SARS and MERS.

How China and HKU SZH deal with COVID-19

Much is unknown about the virus and its nature, though its genome has been identified. From epidemiological data, it is confirmed to be highly infective and yet with an unknown rate of asymptomatic carriers, which can be an undefinable and yet extremely threatening source of transmission of the virus. For those who are affected by the virus, the symptoms are usually fever, dry cough, significant lung changes by CT scans leading to respiratory failures, and death. Mortality is higher in, though not exclusively to, the elderly and those with co-morbid conditions.

There is no known treatment apart from supportive measures such as assisted ventilations by artificial ventilators. No drugs are clinically proven to be effective and no vaccines are available. Therefore, the only way to tackle this outbreak is to reduce the infection rate.

I went back to China on February 3rd 2020 at the peak of the outbreak in China, while the rest of the world was still relatively unaffected. There was widespread fear and for those in Wuhan, even desperation. Hospitals were completely overwhelmed. I witnessed and experienced the huge, resolute, and unprecedented efforts made by the Chinese government nationally and locally, the endurance of the people, the courage of the frontline medical and nursing staff to provide care to the affected patients, often at the risk of their lives, and the moving display of tremendous kindness shown by organisations and individuals alike. The darkest moments could indeed lighten up the brightness of the human spirits.

In this section, I shall attempt to describe, in some detail, how China in general and at HKU SZH in particular dealt with this crisis. What we practised at HKU SZH is part of a national standard. In other words, nearly all hospitals in China adopted the same measures. To start with, since the genome of COVID-19 was known and published by Chinese scientists very early on, a test was developed. A test like this would usually involve a target (either the antigen, from the virus, or an antibody, from the patient's own immunity response), a need for a modern automatic equipment which can handle a large volume of samples, and a standard operating procedure for regular validation for the specificity and sensitivity of the test to ensure its accuracy. Nothing can be done if one of these three is not properly implemented. In general, it is my observation that most hospitals with beds more than 1,000 would have such equipment in China. Once this diagnostic test was developed, the Chinese government identified it as a key plank not only in diagnosis of the infection but even more importantly, in contact tracing, surveillance of individual patients and screening for symptomatic carriers. In the first eight weeks of the outbreak, the Chinese government issued regular updated versions of national guidance in dealing with the virus to all healthcare workers in the country, based on the most up-to-date national data. The tests would be carried out at least three times for any individual patients, more in certain cases. In our own hospital, our own even stricter criteria are that we need three consecutive negative tests before we can declare a patient of being COVID-19 negative. Any positive test will be doubly checked by the Infectious Disease Hospital and triple checked by the National Centre of Diseases Control (NCDC) in China. This intensive use of tests for COVID-19 has been widely applauded by the global health community as one of the main reasons why countries such as China, South Korea, and Germany are successful in suppressing the outbreak, or in common terms, flattening the curve.

Since there is no effective treatment or vaccine for prevention, the only other most effective measures are isolation for the patients and massive public education campaign in promoting universal practice of wearing masks, hand washing, social distancing, and avoidance of public events including the long-cherished Chinese culture of dining out. For instance, in HKU SZH, the canteen was closed but the catering staff kept working. Three meals daily (breakfast, lunch, and dinner) were provided for free to all staff in the initial crisis period, there was no menu, but it would be a balanced meal with meat, eggs, vegetables, and rice. Each department or ward had to notify the hospital catering staff electronically the day before how many breakfasts, lunches, or dinners were needed and these would then be delivered. No one was allowed to eat in groups.

To avoid cross infection between the public and the staff,

outpatients and inpatients clinical services were reduced. Surgical procedures were kept to the minimum, apart from emergencies. Others, such as dental services, oral medicine and ophthalmology, were closed. All patients, before admission, would have to be screened for the virus before attending the wards. All entries and exits in the hospital were modified to form a single and unidirectional path of human flow with each entry point being guarded by staff who checked the temperature of the entrants, no exception allowed. Entry points could not be used as exits and vice versa. So, in a big hospital like HKU SZH with so many main blocks, each block would have its own temperature check point. Car entry points were reduced to one only, elevators use was also curtailed, and some inpatient areas were closed.

Like most hospitals in China, HKU SZH has a fever clinic which was separate from Emergency Room (ER) or the OPD. All patients attending the fever clinic or ER with relevant travelling history would have the COVID test and while waiting for the results, which took about 6-8 hours, the patients were isolated individually in a temporary and self-contained room. If found positive, they would be transferred out to the Infectious Diseases Hospital, escorted by staff with full PPE; and if the first test was negative but they did have symptoms, then they would be admitted to our isolation wards. Four such wards were created, all on the ground floor, with a total capacity of 70 beds. It is a testament of the success of the national and local effort that when I got involved in looking after these wards during this crisis, the total number of patients in isolation was more than 50 and by the time I left for the UK, six weeks later, there were only five patients. One of the most remarkable things was that when these patients had their mandatory chest CT scan within six hours of admission, their passage to the CT scan was completely blocked off to all others by the security guards and was kept apart for at least a distance of 20 metres.

All meetings were cancelled to minimise group gathering. The only meeting was a daily meeting headed by the Hospital Chief Executive who set up a task force consisting of the key personnel and this was held outdoors. An email or a message on the hospital app based on mobile devices is created to request that all staff were mandated to fill in a health declaration form, before 4 p.m. every day. The aim of this was to collect information on the updated health status of all the staff to see if the staff was at work or off work, and if there were the presence of any symptoms such as fever, cough, travelling to other parts of China. During my six weeks, I was late once in filling out this survey and by 7.00 p.m., I got an electronic message notifying me I needed to fill in the information! To avoid wastage of protective personal equipment, masks and caps, each staff was classified based on their clinical duties into high risk groups such as Intensive Care Unit (ICU) and relatively low risk groups such as the office clerical staff. For instance, each Monday I was given a set of masks to use for the whole week. I needed to wear the mask all the time when I was out of my office. The staff, especially the medical and nursing staff, were encouraged to clear their holidays accrued from 2019. This would ensure also that their risk of exposure was kept to the minimum, in line with the national advice for people to stay at home. For essential services such as ER, the fever clinic, and the newly created four isolation wards, there was some relocation of staff to make sure that these essential services were adequately covered. This relocation exercise was successfully implemented within days as many staff members volunteered to work in these high-risk areas. They showed selfless dedication. There was even a team of medical and nursing staff who volunteered to be relocated to the local Infectious Diseases Hospital, which admitted all the confirmed and highly suspected cases. There was also active training program organised by the human resources department and the hospital infection control team for all staff on the proper use of PPE and the updated national guidelines. Other key supporting departments, such as radiology and laboratory, put in extra rosters for round-the-clock CT scanning and the COVID-19 tests for patients from ER and fever clinics. All patients admitted from OPD also had to have the tests done before admission to the wards.

It is therefore a matter of great pride and relief that by the end of March 2020, no front-line medical or nursing staff was reported as being infected at HKU SZH. This was no small achievement. The staff was united in their solidarity and fortitude. They showed remarkable attributes in following the advice laid down by the government and the hospital. Their vigilance of fighting the virus and the desire to help the patients and each other had to be seen to be believed. I was deeply moved.

There were of course some very early teething problems, both nationally and locally. It is the very nature of a viral outbreak, or indeed any outbreak, that one is always caught off guard and even unprepared, however skilled we think we are. This viral outbreak illustrated perfectly that this various degree of unpreparedness is a global phenomenon. The Chinese government, once having ascertained that the outbreak was from a new virus by the middle of January 2020, took decisive and strong actions, mobilising human and material resources in a way which has won international admiration. Volunteers of medical and nursing teams were coordinated to go to and help Wuhan, which was the epicentre. Military personnel, equipped with the necessary hardware, were called to help with transports to ensure a continued and uninterrupted logistical supply of essential materials and food, especially to the lockdown areas. Temporary hospitals of

1,000-bed capacity were quickly built and the manufacturing sector of the country was commissioned to hugely increase their manufacturing capacities for extra medical supplies from ventilators, to caps, PPE, masks, and antiseptics. There were initial shortages of PPE and masks but then after four to six weeks, the shortages were resolved as production was ramped on a scale hardly imaginable before. This is a country where the leaders are willing to lead while the public are willing to be led, with a single aim, to save lives and to protect lives. There was an unanimity of purpose which I have never experienced before.

By the middle of March 2020, both national and local data were beginning to show that the situation was improving with only sporadic cases in various parts of China. Things were beginning to get back to normal. The capacity of all the clinical services at HKU SZH was gradually restored. The HKU SZH OPD attendances, from a high of more than 6,000/day prior to this pandemic, dropped to about 1,000/day as patients chose to stay home. By late March, the HKU SZH OPD attendance has crawled back to more than 4,000/day, around two-thirds of its previous activity. By then other countries were severely affected, once again confirming that this virus is highly effective in its transmission and infectivity. It was South Korea first with major outbreak, then Italy, Iran, and within three weeks, Europe was the epicentre with more deaths than in China. From then on, even though air traffic from Europe and China to the USA was closed, the USA was affected and by the end of March 2020, the USA became the epicentre with the highest number of infected cases and deaths.

The Impact on Health Systems and Services

It was clear by late March 2020 that this crisis is the most severe health crisis the world has ever known since the Spanish Flu crisis in 1918. The world as it then was, not as interconnected as we are now. Globalisation has for the past 20 years been the norm. Therefore, it must be pointed out that in many ways this crisis is more alarming than the Spanish Flu. This is a modern-day globalisation of an almost apocalyptic health crisis within just four months. Although medical advances had been phenomenal and ground-breaking in the last 100 years since the Spanish Flu, the government in each country, with no exception, however rich and advanced the country may be, was caught by the magnitude and the speed of the outbreak to become a pandemic and the havocs that the virus caused. Nearly all countries are paralysed.

No country was able to take decisive action right from the start because so much was unknown about this virus with hardly any previous data for comparison except SARS in 2003 and MERS in 2012. Each country had to take actions based on what was known in this short span of time or what was estimated by the scientists, especially epidemiologists working on mathematical modelling and scenarios. Each country was also constrained by consideration of what measures were acceptable by the public and how each of the health services was equipped and staffed to cope. Some countries, such as the UK, Germany, and the USA, took a graduated and graded approach, calibrated their policies based on cumulated data and events. In China, the government took a commanding and decisive role by having a top down approach based on real time information and data fed from the local and provincial levels. The Chinese government issued no less than six versions of guidelines on how this virus should be dealt with by the health professionals since January and each version represented an updated version adjusted according to the latest epidemiological, scientific, and clinical information. In addition, China also adopted the lockdown approach not only for Wuhan but very soon for the whole of the province of Hubei. This approach, though initially surprising for many other countries, mainly in the West, for its audacity, was later universally admired and was regarded as one of the main reasons for bringing the outbreak under control within three months.

In face of such a rampant outbreak, the other absolutely key essential policy was to prevent the medical services from being completely overwhelmed, such as what was experienced initially in Wuhan, then Italy, then Spain. Even for an advanced country like the USA, the fear was that the medical services would not be able to cope in some major cities like New York, and Chicago, which, similar to Wuhan, are also transportation hubs. The problems faced by all countries are similar. The commonest problems faced by all mainly belong to three areas, as described below.

Firstly, there was severe and acute shortage of adequate supplies of personal protective equipment (PPE) to healthcare workers, such as masks, gowns, caps, gloves. Most of these PPE, to be effective, are designed for single use only and thus have to be disposed of right after their use. The demand and the needs were so grossly mismatched that most exposed front-line staff, such as medical and nursing personnel, were often inadequately provided with enough PPE for their protection in carrying out their work. As a result, there were, sadly, reports of fatalities affecting the medical staff in various countries.

Secondly, there was a severe global shortage of ventilators. Since this virus can cause such rapid and extensive damage to the lungs, only artificial ventilation can sustain human lives before one's own immunity starts to recover to combat the virus. Nearly all the affected countries are not self-sufficient in the supply of ventilators. The only exception is perhaps China or Germany, which is able, through national directives, to increase on a huge scale the production of home-made ventilators. Other countries had to work, often belatedly, with their own home-grown manufacturers, engineers, and scientists to remodel nearly their whole manufacturing base to meet the needs and demands for ventilators. But this process will take time to move into mass production. Therein reflects another structural problem. Most of these advanced economies have long been engaged in climbing up the value chain in chasing the high-end products that a strong manufacturing sector for basic, non glamorous, yet essential products simply does not exist. The long-held principle of Just in Time (JIT) delivery and a smooth globalisation of logistics and supply chains seem to reassure that stocks for these supplies are kept more for replacement and not for new demands. This reflects no fault on each of these countries as the world has indeed enjoyed significant growth to enable a continuous rise in living standards, with part of this due to globalisation and Just in Time model of speedier and smoother logistics in the supply chain. This is best illustrated by how fast an ordered item online can be delivered to the consumer. So nearly all countries are caught short of such essential items, supplies cannot keep up with demands, leading to herd behaviour and scrambling, even by governments. All of a sudden in this pandemic, this great acceleration in growth and prosperity in the past 50 years has become the great deceleration as a result of this pandemic. Everything has to be slowed down except for medical supplies and PPE. Road is preferably kept empty rather than congested.

China may be an exception here. Long since regarded as the Factory of the World, its manufacturing sector has such a strong foundation and flexibility that it was able to respond in such a way that, despite the initial shortage of supplies of PPE and the closing of factories for the Spring Festival holidays for two weeks, this sector was able to catch up with demands that the supplies for China were more or less self-sufficient, and in some cases, even for exports as well. When I left China in late March 2020, there were no shortages.

Thirdly, the tests. To me, it is such a generic word that it needs proper explaining. There is considerable debate in the international press about tests and WHO advises that the key to fighting the virus is to test, test, test. But then, what does test actually mean? The area for heated debate was the issue of testing for the virus. There are two main types of tests to be clarified here. The test for the actual presence of the virus is called the nuclei acid amplification test (NAAT or NAT). This is for the detection and diagnosis for both patients and carriers, especially asymptomatic carriers, mainly using a technique called rt-PCR (reverse transcriptase polymerase chain reaction). This test is vital for contact tracing as well. The best outcome in dealing with the outbreak is to test extensively in both the patients and contacts. This test is a much more technically advanced test as it involves the creation of a primer based on the nuclei acid (either DNA or RNA) of the virus. It involves taking a nasopharyngeal swab or a throat swab. It is commonly known as the antigen test as it tests for the presence of the virus which carries the antigen. It therefore does not depend on the immunity response of the person being tested. This test was the main test used in China and other countries such as South Korea, Singapore, and Germany. In fact, China is the first country that can carry out this test on a massive scale, with reagents produced by a major Shenzhen biotechnology company called the BGI, which was the first in the world to come up with such a NAT test. The other test is for the presence of antibody to the virus. This is a test which is being developed both as a blood test and as a point of care, finger-pricked test. This is technically much simpler, but the detection of the antibody does depend on a normal immune response of the person being tested. Both the test for the virus and the test for the antibody have their advocates but there is a gap in that the NAT can detect the virus before the body can mount a sufficient immune response to produce the antibody in sufficient titres to be detectable. So, the antibody test is host dependent and there is a window of negativity before the immune response can be fully completed. The other mandatory step for both of these tests, which somehow is not properly mentioned in the international press and the public not being properly informed, is that for these tests to be of value and clinically accurate, it will depend on the supplies of the proper reagents used in these tests. The quality of these tests would entirely depend on the reagents and the technical know-how in carrying out such tests. Its reproducibility, precision, and accuracy have to be properly worked out. This quality also has to be approved and certified by national licensing authority in each country. In other words, for both the nucleic acid and the antibody tests, there is a quality standard to be met. An erroneous result can potentially do more damage than no result. Overestimation (false positives) and underestimation (false negatives) must be minimised before such tests, often commercially marketed as kits, can be used for the public. The public must be assured, as an article of faith, that these kits are reliable, accurate, and informative. The worse outcome is an unreliable test leading to erratic action or even panic. Countries as advanced as the USA and the UK are now finding it extremely difficult to come up with a test of such quality to be used on a massive scale to satisfy the demands of the public, despite both countries boasting to house some of the most advanced high-tech biomedical giants. So even when WHO advises that the key to control of this endemic is to test, test, and test, most countries are unable to do so in such a short period of time because of lack of supply of the necessary reagents and lack of standards of how to ensure uniformity of the test and its results.

If these logistical problems about supplies, reagents, and standards can be resolved, then one can aim for a public-health-orientated and long-term policy by doing both tests for the diagnosis, contact tracing, and assessment of immunity status on the basis of an epidemiological study to assess the immunity status of the population. The ideal finding would be one who is antigen negative but antibody positive, which means that this person is protected, having been previously exposed, and can be freed from social isolation. This first group, in my view, may turn out to be the largest group in any population study. If the result shows antibody negative and antigen positive, then this infection can be a symptomatic case or an asymptomatic case (estimated to be affecting up to 25% of infected patients). As such, they should be isolated, and contact tracing initiated. This group can be considered for specific antiviral treatment if and when available, or enrolment into ethically approved clinical trial for early pre-emptive interventional treatment drug trial. If the tests show both antibody and antigen are negative, then this group can be actively considered for immunisation by a COVID-19 vaccine, if available. For the second and the third groups, given the current fast tracked and global race in clinical trials on new, antiviral treatments and the development of a vaccine, it is likely that both can be available in less than two years' time.

Common Global Efforts

Despite the problems listed above which most countries are facing, there are also some commonalities that are almost universally agreed and now practised. It stems from the principle that the virus cannot survive outside the human bodies for long and therefore the best way to stop the transmission from one individual to another is social distancing and self-isolation. These are now the buzzword in the archives of glossaries originated from this pandemic. The rationale here is very simple. If we stop interacting with other people in any crowds, any groups, any social events and only restrict ourselves to be at home with our own families, then our risk of infection would be significantly reduced since we are much less exposed to droplet of virus from other people. Furthermore, this social distancing can even be enhanced by, say, if we do need to go out to get essential supplies such as food, not only we can wear masks, but we should keep a safe distance from others, as the virus, being a droplet, cannot travel far in the air before it falls to the ground. The recommendation would be two metres apart, which is now not only practised widely in the UK, but by many other countries as well.

By the collective and sustained efforts of all the individuals in practising social isolation, there will thus be a collective gain in the reduction of overall cases and hence the medical services can avoid being overwhelmed. Such measures are based on an easy-to-understand principle and common sense, and easy to practise. Although inconvenient at times for some perhaps, it will gain collective good. These measures can further be enhanced by the closure of restaurants, pubs, clubs, sporting events, non-essential retail shops, and the avoidance of public gatherings. Even education institutions are closed. People are encouraged to work from home, and, at this time of the pandemic, there is no better argument than the saying that home is the safest place to be. These measures are now the standards in nearly all countries. The great divergence in human behaviour is now becoming the great convergence. Initially, there was some complacency about this sort of behaviour advice in the West, especially among the young people, since it has been viewed as impinging on their liberty and freedom of movements. However, video footages shown in the UK, of carefree crowds in the parks on a sunny day and pubs being full in the evenings as if nothing has happened, stirred up a public outcry against such behaviour, regarded as selfish and ill considerate. Since the video clips broadcast and, together with the fact that the data showed that the young are just as commonly infected as the elderly, there was an immediate and noticeable improvement in their attitude and behaviour. The UK, from what I can see, is now a quiet country, from Mondays to Sundays. It used to be quiet only on Christmas Day, now it is quiet every day.

The Debate on Herd Immunity

With all the new words coming out from this pandemic, herd immunity is by far the most controversial and deserves some explanation. The words were first used in public in the UK press when it reported that the UK government's initial response was to move towards an achievement of herd immunity. The thinking for this Darwinian approach is that since the virus pandemic has happened and it is much too late to stop it, and since the mortality is reasonably low, especially in the young, it may be an option that, if the society lets the virus run its course, as it will, then at the end of this process most people, called the herd, would have acquired the immunity to protect this herd and to prevent them from spreading infection to others. The attainment of such a herd immunity will be beneficial in the long term but it does mean more people will die from the infection in the short term if this pandemic is allowed to run its course. In short, this school of thought advocates that since resources are limited, it is better to have graded isolation and protection of the elderly, the very young, and those with co-morbid medical conditions. It is like a risk stratified, targeted approach. Meanwhile, let the healthy and the young develop this herd immunity. The counter argument against this is the other mainstream school of thought, and it is known as the Total Lockdown approach to break the transmission, best evidenced in China, which claimed success in barely under 12 weeks. Both schools of thoughts sound plausible, herd immunity may show long-term gain while lockdown approach may be unsustainable in the long term. This debate, though not drawn to a conclusion, does seem to be tilting towards the side of lockdown approach, and the UK government, having initially explored this herd immunity approach, has also come down on the fence of the lockdown approach. In fact, depending on how one's own view is from, both schools of thoughts are correct, and they do not have to be mutually exclusive. Indeed, they should be and can be mutually inclusive depending on at what stage the pandemic is at. My own view is that this herd immunity, at least for now and in these days of global travel and human movements, is difficult for the time being as it is not possible to define the meaning of a herd in the modern world of vast global movements of people on a daily basis. Is it the local indigenous population or does it apply to those new comers and goers too? Is the herd defined by national borders? This herd immunity, given its scientific merits and the sound principle of having one's own immunity to ward off the virus, should be better thought through first to enable the global community to agree on a broad and general international consensus to define what herd in modern days means.

Masks - To Use or Not To Use

Strangely, if there is one issue which is causing significant anxiety, debate, and uncertainties currently, and which reflects the difference in cultures and people's behaviour between East and West, it would be on the use of surgical masks. The original purpose of surgical masks, as the name suggests, was to protect surgeons when they go into the operating theatre. In other words, for reducing infection through breathing, as opposed to other masks such as those for cosmetic purposes like the Venetian Masks worn in the annual Carnival of Venice!

Having spent six weeks in Shenzhen during the most trying time in China, and now going through an equally trying time in the UK, I cannot help but notice the difference in attitude between the East and the West. This difference can best be described as the difference in the perceived benefits on the use of masks.

The use of masks for the protection of air pollution has always been accepted as a norm for the daily lives of the people in some Asian countries such as China, Japan, Singapore, and South Korea. Following the lessons learned in the outbreak of SARS in 2003, from which the public is deeply scarred, the use of masks for personal protection from transmission of diseases has become habitual and even serves as a model of good practice. The public in these countries, in times of any viral outbreak, is distinctly noticeable by how compliant they are and how universal this practice is. Wherever you go and whoever you meet, people are wearing masks in these times. In fact, you will get a strange look from the others if you don't use one. So, in short, the need and the use of masks in times of an outbreak are the social norm, acceptable, and practised by all in countries like China, Japan, and Korea.

Before I went back to Shenzhen in early February 2020, I had to search for some masks in the UK, with great difficulty, prior to my trip. I knew I had to protect myself and others in doing my work in Shenzhen. In the beginning, masks were in short supply in China too and our hospital had to ration its use so no one was found wanting. At the peak of the shortage, our staff even worked voluntarily over the weekends and evenings to produce self-made masks. When I went to see them in their work room, working diligently away one Friday evening, I was truly moved, because it reflected such a determined attitude in working out our own solution. None of the staff was an engineer by background, they simply learned all about protective masks through the internet. Whether it is truly protective was another matter, what matters was it demonstrated in unambiguous terms their reliance on self-sufficiency and willingness in coming up with a solution to produce, however a limited number of masks it may be, to help their colleagues in the hospital.

Yet, I also remembered very clearly, when I was departing for the UK on March 16th 2020, that, apart from us Asians, no other passengers in any departure gates in Hong Kong International Airport were wearing any masks, despite the HKSAR governmental advice. This advice was clearly ignored by the non-Asians. I could hardly believe what I saw, as if this international airport was divided into two camps. The Asians all wearing masks while the non-Asians weren't, strolling about in a nonchalant, carefree manner that one could only admire or ridicule. I actually asked one of the staff why these people were not told to wear masks, and their reply to me was that the staff did tell them but none of them took any notice, gesturing that it was of no proven benefits. There was nothing anyone could do as they all had their boarding passes. The difference in attitude is even more stark when I got back to the UK which was, by then, already heading for a lockdown mode. Only a few of British people in public wore masks and the UK government, in issuing their advice, has not advised the public to wear masks throughout the whole period. To be fair, even WHO did not advocate the widespread use of masks. It only advised that masks should be worn by those who have symptoms or those involve in patients care.

So should masks be used at times like this? As the immortal line in the Shakespeare play *Hamlet* said: "To be or not to be, that is the question!" My view is that wearing a mask serves three main purposes. First, to protect one from spreading germs to others if one sneezes or coughs. The second one is not dissimilar to the first one, and that is, to make sure others have less chance of passing germs to us. The message is also sent that if one coughs or sneezes, the protection works both ways. Let us ask ourselves one question. For example, would we be comfortable if we are stuck in a lift or a plane, and the chap next to us keeps coughing or sneezing without a mask at times like this? The answer is indisputably obvious. The third one is symbolic but equally important in nature. It sends out clear messages to all others that we take this protection very seriously. It fosters trust in each other and enhances a sense of civic responsibility. Everyone knows the importance of hand washings. By not wearing a mask, one can assume that hand washings may not be taken seriously by that someone. By wearing a mask, it will create the opposite impression. So, this is a signal to others you are doing your bit to protect them and therefore, they should do so likewise.

While these arguments above have not been proven conclusively by medical or epidemiological studies, most countries in the West do not advocate strongly the use of masks, though no one advises against it. It is left to the individual to decide. There is a cultural attitude that wearing protective masks in public may be seen as socially odd. Only some, such as butchers, painters, and decorators, wear masks. And Superman in a film wearing a mask or Michael Jackson wearing a mask in public certainly would not raise any eyebrows. There is now, however, the beginning of an honest debate in the West on this and I can already discern a major shift in the attitude towards the necessity of wearing a mask. Articles and opinions have been published in respectable newspapers in various countries advocating, on balance, that wearing a mask will be beneficial. The rationale for this is very simple. If this is good and important for the healthcare workers to protect themselves by wearing masks, why should the public not wear masks? Protecting should be for all and at these times of crisis, there is simply no worthy argument against wearing masks for any cosmetic, social, or cultural reasons.

To my own satisfaction, this fundamental difference between the East and the West has gradually changed and people are now beginning to accept the necessity of wearing masks in barely the three weeks since I arrived back in the UK on March 17th. On March 30th, Austria became the first country in Europe telling the people to wear masks when shopping. The need for this is now adopted in Germany and France. WHO is said to be actively considering updating its guidelines on the use of masks. The USA, as of April 2020, are already recommending the use of masks by the public. It is therefore hard not to draw the impression that one of the key reasons that China and Korea are successful in containing the infection is the general use of masks by the public.

The next big challenge, however, having accepted the needs and the necessities of masks for the public good, is the problem of ensuring supplies meeting the demands. After all, the making of masks is regarded as a low tech, low skill, and low profit margin piece of manufacturing, so the making of surgical masks in most advanced economies has been dished out to other countries. This is now a major and acute problem worldwide. It is now estimated that at least one third of the world population (about three billion) are in lockdown mode. Assuming even one mask per person per day is needed, the production targets from the manufacturer will be staggering, there simply is no manufacturing capacity to satisfy the demand if these people are advised to wear masks. Most of the masks in the world are made in China and countries in the East. China, Japan, and South Korea are self-sufficient in producing adequate masks for their own people. If, however, countries in the West advocate the use of masks, then the supply will simply be dried up within days. It is therefore possible, predictable even, that these countries can only restrict the use of masks in the hospital settings because of the certain knowledge that any such advice to the public will lead to mass hysteria and panic in searching for a mask. So, it is better not to advise on the undeliverable and unachievable. I do feel that there should be a calm, reasoned, and international appraisal at some stage to address this problem to reach a common consensus. It may not be possible to reach consensus due to cultural attitude but nevertheless, it should at least be looked at and the need properly debated. While this debate goes on, it is interesting to point out that in the East, designer-type or personalised masks are already on the market for purchase so one can match the scarf or the outfit with a coloured mask, pattern mask, or logo mask, not dissimilar to buying an Apple Watch with a chosen wrist band collection of various colours to match the occasion and the outfit. In fact, I have seen newspaper reports on recent fashion shows in the Far East where the models walked on the catwalk with masks of different colours and patterns to match the latest fashion. So we can turn the argument upside down by seeing this not only as health protection but also as a personal accessory and expression of trendiness to be used when and where necessary!

What Next - From Diversity to Uniformity

Over the last few decades, there have been unprecedented technological advances in the medical field for diagnostics and treatments, with the biomedical sector long seen as one of the growth areas. Yet this crisis has painfully exposed us to see the folly of this thinking. We have overlooked the importance of basic but essential supplies in medical fields such as masks, antiseptics, PPE, and simple non-invasive ventilators. We have been caught swimming in a receding tide without our trunks. I reminded myself that the USA has long had a policy on national security that there would be a strategic oil reserve for 90 days in case of global oil shortage or war. The time has arrived perhaps for each country to have a similar model of precaution in dealing with future outbreaks by building up a similar strategic reserve of essentials of such low-cost but life-saving items as these for 90 days or at least have the manufacturing capacity of producing more at short notice, just like China did in January and February 2020, despite the long break for the Spring Festival holiday (Lunar New Year). These 90 days of manufacturing nuances will be vital in helping each country to buy valuable time in coming up with the right solution while protecting the public at the same time.

The last few months can perhaps be described as, in the words of Charles Dickens, "It was the best of times, it was the worst of times." The times for deep fear and the times for solidarity. The world has been turned upside down, political ideology on big governments and small governments has a complete turnaround, individual liberty and community needs are completely redressed, the commonly accepted economic model of growth, of market needs instead of human needs, is changed beyond recognition. A global crisis which knows of no boundaries or ideology needs a global solution. G7 and G20 countries are now unanimous in working together for a common approach to deal with the crisis, commonality is now the prevailing attitude. We are all in this together, exceptions will not be exceptions anymore. In the final analysis, it may indeed take an apocalyptic crisis like COVID-19 for humanities to come together, and diversity becomes uniformity, a triumph for the human spirits.

PART 4:

MY RECOLLECTIONS AND REFLECTIONS

CHAPTER 26

An Overseas Chinese

I first learned of the word diaspora when I arrived in the UK in 1980. The definition of a diaspora is the dispersion of people from their homeland or a community formed by people who have exited or been removed from their homeland. An example of a diaspora is a community of Jewish people settled together after they were dispersed from another land. It quickly dawned on me that there is a Chinese diaspora too and in fact, the Chinese diaspora is by far the biggest in the world, estimated to be around 50 million ethnic Chinese living outside mainland China, Taiwan, Hong Kong, and Macao. These overseas Chinese are known as '*huaqiao*' in *putonghua*. The main difference between the Jewish and Chinese diaspora is that the Jewish diaspora has its origin thousands of years ago and were exiled, forced to live somewhere in the absence of their own nation state, while the Chinese diaspora is a relatively recent event by comparison. Most of the Chinese migration to other countries happened in the 19th and 20th centuries. People left China to escape from wars, starvation, and poverty. The first generation of Chinese immigrants made a living by blood, sweat, and tears while culturally they never quite tried to integrate with the host countries, preferring to live instead in their own communities, hence the creations of China Towns in so many parts of the world. Their purpose for such an exit from homeland was not only to earn some money to send back to their poor and starving families in China, but also to prepare the second or future generations for a proper education which they themselves lacked. Thus, they often lived their lives very frugally with very meagre means. They demonstrated great resilience and endurance. I admire them for their fortitude, especially in difficult times. I see myself as one of Chinese diaspora although I am lucky enough to be one of the newer ones, freed from the sufferings of my predecessors. I have a yearning to go back to my roots, to go back to the country of my birth, and in so doing, to taste what life in China is like, to get to know China better. This yearning for going back to one's roots tends to happen to all those who have emigrated, very much like the US citizens of Irish or Italian ancestry who develop an intense interest in Ireland or Italy, both countries being well-known for their first-generation immigrants to the USA.

Yearning for My Heritage

Ever since the age of three, my experience of China has always been limited, apart from the few occasions of going back to China with my family as tourists, seeing the sights and sampling the cuisine the ways tourists do. Yet I have always felt very deeply the Chinese heritage in me. I have hoped that my Chinese heritage can be a benchmark for me to judge and understand myself better. Having worked and lived in the UK for more than 30 years, I may have a fair idea of how others judge me in the UK, but I do not know how I will be judged as a Western-trained ethnic Chinese doctor working in China. When I was in Hong Kong during my early years of education, I was made aware of the upheavals of the major political movements such as the Great Leap Forward and the Cultural Revolution. These were the early events in China that I can remember, having been taught relatively little in recent Chinese history in school. The other seminal event was the Hong Kong riots in 1967 when Hong Kong was on the verge of being handed back to China if the British colonial administration was not able to regain control of public order. My school was closed for a very short period due to public danger.

Views from Life in the UK

These events eventually passed and by the time I arrived in the UK in 1980, China had just launched the new reform and opening-up policy, initiated by Deng Xiaoping. At the time, I felt very excited about my Chinese heritage and decided to keep myself abreast of developments and events. This is because not only do I not know much about Chinese history but of more importance is that being Chinese in the UK, the British would quite naturally see me as an ethnic Chinese and ask me about my views on China and Hong Kong, especially since Hong Kong was the last remaining jewel in the Crown left from the British Empire days. The British, quite naturally, viewed China and Hong Kong with much interest and sentiment.

So while being trained as a haematologist in the UK, I started to read books on China, mostly in English, written in those days mainly by scholars in the USA, though latterly UK too. Reading these books gave me a basis of understanding China through the eyes of Westerners, but it still left me with a somewhat detached view, I realised that there were gaps to be filled. So I followed news from China, especially on its economic developments and its reforms programmes.

Of particular topical interest while I was in the UK was the discussion between China and the UK on the future of Hong Kong post 1997. The discussion was widely covered by the international press, especially when Deng Xiaoping came up with the One Country, Two Systems concept. It is also worth pointing out that one of the first significant actions that The People's Republic of China (PRC) undertook on becoming a permanent member of the Security Council of the United Nations way back in 1971, was to register with the United Nations that the Treaty of Nanking, signed in 1842 in which Hong Kong was ceded to the UK, was an unequal treaty. At the beginning of the reforms in China, the then governor of Hong Kong, the late Lord MacLehose, went to Beijing for a visit and had a meeting with Deng Xiaoping, who then relayed to the UK the intention of China to take back Hong Kong.

During this period of opening up China to the outside world and major reforms, I was also able to meet many professional people from mainland China at the hospital I worked in. Being a university hospital, it welcomed many Chinese from the mainland as research scientists. Some of whom became my colleagues and friends. Through them I got to rekindle my cultural heritage, appreciate the national traits such as fondness of good food and willingness for hard work. I also noticed that they were very well-informed about worldly affairs. I felt somewhat inadequate and questioned myself why I was less informed about China than they were about the UK. I started to watch TV shows, documentaries, and news from TV stations based in China. I found these programmes immensely helpful, informative, and enjoyable. During this same period, as China emerged on the world stage, the sheer size of its population and its long civilisation also stimulated widespread interest from the West, so there were many well produced documentaries from the UK too. I found these documentaries by and large fairly impartial, helping me greatly in my quest for understanding China from viewpoints both of China and the UK. Also at the same time, I also had access to CGTN which produced many first-class documentaries, and to name just a few, such as the *Origins and Civilization along the Yangtze River*, *The Rise of the Great Powers in the Last 500 Years* (a first-class documentary series of 11 episodes tracing the origin of Western powers based on their political, economic and scientific developments), and *History of China from Dynasty to Dynasty*.

The Moments of Pride

Two important dates needed special mention. The first was July 1st 1997 when Hong Kong was officially handed back to China under the Joint Declaration by the Chinese and the UK governments which stated that the administration of Hong Kong will be based on the Basic Law under the One Country, Two Systems principle for 50 years. I watched this historic event live on TV at home in Liverpool. It was a rainy day, not only in Hong Kong but in Liverpool too! I saw the official ceremony of the Hong Kong handover to China with the UK flag being lowered, the Chinese flag being raised, and national anthems being played, attended by both the President of China and the Prime Minister of the UK, senior officials and dignitaries. It was sobering and solemn. The scene that was as clear in my mind now as then was when the last Governor of Hong Kong, Chris Patten, boarded with his family onto the Royal Britannia on her last official voyage back to the UK. The next day, I also saw on TV the Chinese leaders witnessing the swearing in ceremony of the first Chief Executive of the Hong Kong Special Administrative Region (HKSAR, which was from then on the official name of Hong Kong). I thought I was watching history in the making. I was very moved, overcome with pride, and felt that a line has been drawn under the Opium War. Hong Kong has gone back to its motherland. It is also a very distinctive and remarkable chapter in the history of British colonialism, as never before a colony was handed back to its mother country in the history of the world. Hong Kong has started a new beginning. Personally, the event also left me with a great feeling of nostalgia and a certain degree of sadness, seeing myself as a product of the British colonial system from childhood to adulthood, from a student to a professional, all started from my move to Hong Kong from China at the age of three. I felt an immense gratitude to the British system, reminding myself I may not be what I am today without that system.

The other date was the Beijing Olympics in 2008, the first Olympics China has ever hosted. It confirmed to the whole world the coming of age of modern China, being welcomed into the global community of nations. The opening ceremony was so well choreographed, so rich in portraying the Chinese culture and so dazzling in its portrayal of the diversity of its ethnicities (the national census in 2000 stated there are 56 ethnic groups)! It was a jaw-dropping performance, perfectly and flawlessly played out in the newly built, architecturally beautiful stadium known affectionately as the Bird's Nest (bird's nest is one of the most precious and nutritious cuisines in Chinese culture). This event filled me with huge pride, almost with tears in my eyes. Winning any gold medals or the position in the medal ranking was no longer of any importance. What really was significant was that after nearly 30 years of reform, China has arrived and successfully been restored at the world stage. Much has been written about it being the most expensive and glamorous display of opening ceremonies in the history of the Olympics. I took a different view. It is not how much it cost nor how spectacular it was that counts. What it really displayed was how much effort, how much innovation, how much rehearsal and depth the artistic creation the Chinese people have shown in playing the perfect host to people from all parts of the world with the motto: One World, One Dream. It gives the descriptive words 'meticulous planning, leaving nothing to chance' an entirely new meaning.

So it was with a combination of personal effort in reading, studying, in establishing friendships, in watching the news, and appreciating popular culture that I overcame the early ignorance of China. Curiosity and an eagerness to find out more got the better of me. Even though I was far away from China, I felt I was better informed, maybe even better prepared, to debate and discuss, with a degree of confidence, with my friends and colleagues on issues about China. I have enjoyed these debates and discussions with people from different backgrounds, as these tend not only to focus my views, but also offer me a much wider perspective. Yet, with all my effort, such is the randomness of events, and perhaps even providence, that I was given the chance to learn more, experience more and understand more about China by coming back to work in China in my own chosen profession! Could it be that once again, just like the British colonial system in Hong Kong prepared me as a doctor, that life in the UK for over 30 years prepared me for another professional career in China? It seems almost like that, all the past years have prepared me, in a full circle, for my last big job!

CHAPTER 27

My Rewards

Rewards can mean different things to different people at different stages in life. These can be short term and obvious, like air miles for frequent flyers, or they can be long term and motivating, such as promotion to a higher position in one's career. So, I found myself asking myself repeatedly: do I find my eight years of working in China at HKU SZH rewarding and if the answer is yes, how should I explain it?

Rewards and awards are two different things. Awards can be nominated by others or self-nominating, it involves open recognition and praise, thus it does appeal to one's vanity as it is always nice to have your work recognised by others, especially your own peers. It is a form of public recognition of good work done. Rewards can be different. Being given an award can be rewarding but feeling rewarded does not necessarily mean being awarded by something, such as a medal, a certificate, a membership of a prestigious society or granted admission to an elite club. Awards are something which is both tangible and demonstrative while rewards can often be an enlightened state of feelings. The feeling of being rewarded is best and most gratifying if it comes from the inner self. If it is a rewarding feeling in the heart, then it will always stay in the heart, and will never be taken away.

My Transformative and Humbling Years

For my eight years in China, I have faced challenges, difficulties, often with sleepless nights and anxiety attacks. Friends are all telling me without failing that my hair is getting greyer and greyer by the day. Yet at the same time, I feel rejuvenated by the challenges, feel energised in getting the job done, feel that the targets, however hard, are reachable. The journey is rough, sometimes even stormy, but the destiny is worth every moment of hardship endured. In this process, I have worked with wonderful colleagues, some of them have become friends. The really gratifying thing is that when I first came, we did not have any haematology doctors apart from me. Unlike other hospitals and corporations where newly appointed senior executives or professors often bring their own team of staff as the nucleus of the new team, I did not have that luxury, nor did I think it was the right way to approach things either, so I came alone all the way from the UK. But then I also had the advantage of starting with a clean sheet of paper, without any historical luggage or preconceived prejudices.

We (the haematology department) now have a team of 11 doctors, some seniors, some juniors. I knew none of them before they came, and they did not know each other either. It takes a while for all of us to get used to working with each other. This hotchpotch of haematologists from different parts of China has now developed into a team, a team which can be open and friendly with each other, and in so doing, we all learn together as times go by. The other thing I get from them, and all my friends and colleagues in China and HKU SZH, is a sense of their vitality, a sense of this being a very spirited and vibrant group, which wants to do things in a way which is different from the traditional way they were used to. Vitality is something you can feel when it is there but hard to describe. Being with them spurs me on.

One of my favourite stories to tell was my ward rounds, which I conduct twice weekly, when every inpatient is seen and greeted. Often when I first started, years ago, the frequent question from the medical staff to me was: what chemotherapy should we give for this patient who failed to respond to first line therapy? I never gave them straight away my views or answers but instead I always replied: what do you think we should do? Initially they were not used to it as they were so used to following instructions. So my question always led to a stunned silence, with me not knowing for sure whether they were too afraid to speak, not feeling confident to speak, or even that they were so used to following instructions? Yet after a while, they started to prepare the ward round by anticipating my standard practice of answering a question from them with a question from me. So what they now do is to carry out the necessary literature search themselves or discuss among themselves prior to the ward round. They now are all used to giving me a view during the ward round, backed up by the published information and data they could find. They now know my style, so they cleverly always think of the various possible answers before they ask me a question. This gradually would lead to better teamwork and openness, something which we all value. Everyone can have a view, as long as the view is backed up by facts and figures. I think they do enjoy these ward rounds too, which offer some intellectual vigour to all of us!

I see all my colleagues in our department as our main assets. They can be the medical staff, the assistants, the nurses, and the technical staff. I value them all. The best way to treat assets is to harness them, to get to know them, and to show them that you do care for them, maximise their strength, and help them with their weaknesses. The turnover rate over the years for our medical and technical staff so far is zero. Some of them could have moved to other institutions for promotion and salary enhancement, but they have chosen to stay. This show of loyalty is something I am truly proud of. Choosing to stay can be the ultimate form of endorsement.

A Touching Change of Attitudes

One area which warrants special mention is the haematopoietic stem cell transplant services (HSCT) for which I had been focusing, planning, and developing in the last eight years at HKU SZH. The HSCT is to help cure or control some fatal blood cancers. This service was commissioned in June 2016, and we have now since carried out just over 100 HCSTs. One type of such HSCT requires a donor and the best result is from a tissue compatible (HLA typing) sibling donor called allogeneic HSCT. However, the availability of such an HLA compatible donor is only one in four among siblings, so the more brothers and sisters the patient has, the more chance of a compatible HLA donor. This, for a small size family, can limit its use. In the developed countries, shortage of donors can be rectified by haematologists like me searching on an international HSCT registry service for potential willing donors who have their HLA typing tested and who are registered donors, just like those of us who are registered for blood donation. They will be ready to donate either their bone marrow or their peripheral blood cells. This use of peripheral blood is through the technique called apheresis, which is to operate an automatic cell separation machine to select the right amount of stem cells. This is nowadays more popular and is globally acceptable as it alleviates the need for the donors to have a general anaesthesia to have their bone marrow harvested.

In China, because of the One Child Policy, the chance of a sibling donation for HSCT is very limited so the alternative is through voluntary donation by willing donors. There is now a nationwide government-run agency called the China Bone Marrow Registry of voluntary donors who already have had their HLA typing done with the results stored in the data bank of the Registry, ready to be available to assist registered HSCT centres like ours to search for HLA compatible donors. However, once the donor, be it a related sibling or an unrelated donor, has heard that bone marrow donation may be needed as well, for which they have to undergo general anaesthesia, then it is quite common for them to refuse donation. This reason is mainly cultural, as people in China tend to think of bone marrow cells as too precious to donate, and thus donation will harm the well-being of the donor. This is medically not correct, as the bone marrow cells in a healthy person tend to regenerate, just like our own red cell productions will recover after we donate blood. Because of this, at HKU SZH, we mainly ask the tissue-compatible siblings or Registry for donors in China for their blood cells and not bone marrow. We have now performed quite a number of this volunteer donation and have gone to various parts of China, including Taiwan, to collect such cells to perform successful HSCTs. These donors are often very happy and feel very rewarded that they are helping actively to save someone else's life somewhere in China. The practice and cultural shift in donation of the blood cells and not needing the marrow cells will play a major part of the success and wider application of HSCT in China. I feel very privileged, with immense personal satisfaction, that I am able to play my small part in bringing about the shift in attitude in the last few years. It gave me a small sense of achievement.

So in short, my answer to my own question is that yes, I do feel very rewarded in a way I could never have imagined when I first arrived in HKU SZH in August 2012. I have also learned and developed much more, both as a person and a professional in the last eight years than any other parts of my life.

CHAPTER 28

The Future

It is never easy, if not impossible, to forecast the future, none of us can! No one can look into the crystal ball and come up with predictions though often people do! So I will, for what it is worth, proceed to make some statements, but not to be regarded as predictions. These statements are focused around the rapid technological advances and their impact on the way we live, including medical advances, and how we can best embrace and live with them.

Given the jaw-dropping progress in technology in all aspects of our daily life, from the very minute, such as how our genes can be spliced and re-edited, to the wonderful and weird suggestion on how one day we can book our flight to the moon, one can thus safely think of some reasonable scenarios, not based on the imagination of science fiction but based on what is currently possible.

Need to Cope and Accept Changes

The first is our habitual willingness and tendency to change and adapt (as stated in Darwin's *Theory of Natural Selection*). Those who do not change are sometimes labelled as old-fashioned, conservative 'dinosaurs'. Extinction happens when a species dies out from cataclysmic events, evolutionary problems, or human interference. Let us take mobile phones for example. Years ago, mobile phones used by the public looked, quite ridiculously, like an army walkie-talkie. Those who carried with them such an odd-looking gadget even viewed this as a statement of trendiness. To be seen carrying such a big bulky gadget was regarded then as trendy and a symbol of high achievement or in a position of some importance. However, things are moving so fast that these days, mobile phones are regarded as one of the essential items to be carried with us. They are no longer regarded as a trendy statement but quite possibly more valued than a pocket wallet. Furthermore, by the time one masters all the multiple functionalities of the latest pocket smartphone, such as iPhone 10, its battery will have slowed down so much after such intense use that one will be planning for a new iPhone 11 or even 12. The marketing is now so clever and the development so rapid that, on the average of a three years span, one will be inclined to buy the latest model. Similarly, in the field of medicine, every time a new diagnostic technology or drug becomes available or widely used on a clinical basis, there is almost a guarantee that there is already an alternative and newer cutting-edge research on another replacement drug being published in peer reviewed academic journals. The more reputable the journal is, the more information there is. In short, it means by the time I start to use a new anticancer drug, there will be work undertaken on its replacement, just like smartphones. Therefore, one can assume in the near future, one may have to keep on running just to keep up.

Making Technology the Driver for Human Benefits

The second statement is that these technology breakthroughs will undoubtedly change the way we live and in some cases, enhance personal safety (such as driverless cars or smart home security systems), or make our life much more convenient (24/7 online shopping and delivery, including groceries), much better connected with our loved ones and friends (live video streaming). This will enable us to cocoon ourselves in our comfort zones, if we wish, and remain connected with the outside world, through digital means by various forms of amazing technologies, whenever we feel like socialising or engaging with others. Being sociable now has a new meaning. One can still be regarded as very sociable even without leaving one's room. So safety, convenience, and even sociability are now enhanced by technology.

Take for example driverless, electric cars. This may seem like science fiction a decade ago. Driving currently involves humans using our cerebral ability to coordinate, with a licence, to steer the cars/buses/lorries in different directions with the help of road signs, traffic lights, and dashboard control. Most modern cars even have the help of GPS, but it does not help to reduce accidents, which may be due to drivers' mistakes or worse still, drivers losing concentration, being distracted, being drunk, or even wilfully violating traffic regulations. In other words, the driver is still in control of the vehicle. With the help of AI algorithms, big data, and its interaction with 5G of instant transmission of data, and widespread use of CCTV, GPS, and robotics, a driverless car will be conceivably much safer on the road as this robotic car will be fully aware of the other robotic cars, it is no longer the intention and action of the driver that matters, but rather the information that an integrated software process integrating traffic conditions, weather conditions, and pedestrian movements, all in an instant. They can see around the corners (blind spots) which we humans simply can't. Such cars are already being tested on the roads. It won't be too long before we see them on our roads. Not only are they driverless, they will also be electric, with them comes a major impact in reducing the carbon footprint on our environment.

It would equally be possible to ponder what other aspects of our life such technological advance can or will do for me as a practising clinician. I have already read articles predicting that the medical profession can be seen as being part of a sunset industry. However experienced, hardworking, or conscientious I am in my work, I can never compete with AI, big data, and the supercomputer. They work infinitely faster than the synapses of our neurons in our brain, no matter how bright we are. My areas of weakness and oversights are guaranteed to be covered by them. So what am I to do in this sunset industry called the practice of medicine? The one thing I am left with in my favour, and that is our trump card too, is that, in dealing with the patients, I can offer the human touch and empathy which so far machines cannot do. Indeed, this is what a doctor should and can do. I have often taught my student doctors that in the near future, we may not need to show how smart or knowledgeable we are, the machines will always have the upper hand in this. Yet we can trump the machines on how we care and empathise with the patients, which a machine can never do. In other words, we trump them with our attitude, our endeavour to do good while the machine is only doing what it is programmed to do. Furthermore, some people, myself included, would tend to argue for the importance of human emotional connectivity with others in this modern technology-driven world, this emotional connection is part of our DNA, so it would surely outweigh the notion of AI initiated perfectibility and improvability in this otherwise imperfect world. Because what we are, above all else, is human first and human last. The furthest AI can reach so far is deep learning but it is still far from replacing what is known as the cognitive side of our human brain, even though I am sure there are currently scientists working on it. The old saying that medicine is not only a branch of science but the practice of it is an art, has never been so true in these days of AI, big data, and 5G.

So what are we left to do? We can now foresee that we do not need to drive, we possibly do not need to see a doctor (even some surgeries are now carried out by robotics). We probably do not need to shop at the groceries since goods can be delivered, we certainly do not need to cook as programmed food processors can see to that. We do not need to decide what is on the TV to watch. I am sure the minute we cast our eye on a blank screen, the visual contact from the TV would activate an analysis of our own viewing habits, to continue on an episode of a TV drama we have been watching, and present a list of our preferred programmes on the screen. We do not need to even press any button on any gadget, we only need to say the words or look at it, and it will be done! It is scary, spooky even, but it is plausible. The tools at our disposal will be incredibly intelligently designed machines to offer us maximal comfort, convenience, and safety but it would create and even encourage laziness, thus sacrificing our imagination. Even our intelligence may be eroded due to the lack of effort and thinking.

The Importance of Bridging the Trust Gap

With all these wonderful technological advances in the near future, can there be a darker side? One issue, which in my view has not been adequately addressed, is that these technological advances can only be made, in this global village we live in, based on trust and not suspicions, based on the ideal for human benefits and not their potential misuse. And yet, often it is precisely the potential misuse of these advances and the demonstration of their might that are being explored by nations in their quest for domination or military success in a conflict. For example, in the early 20th century scientists discovered atomic energy, but it was used by the military to turn it into the production of a weapon of mass destruction, and it had been used in war where thousands suffered instant death or for those who survived, may develop cancer later. So, in this global village, there should be trust and good will on all sides. This trust should be, first and foremost, between individuals, then between institutions, and then between nations. This trust is none more so relevant today in the application of technological advances as the production of these machines and their software involves many participants from different institutions and different countries. Machines may be accurate and precise, but these machines cannot tell us who or what to trust, only humans can! This trust, or the lack of it, in this fiercely competitive techno world, can be misplaced, leading to political misinterpretations, fuelling further mistrust. Intellectual property should indisputably be respected but equally this should not be misused as a shield for monopoly of knowledge. Knowledge is only knowledge when it is shared. Nor should the respect for intellectual property be used as a tool to condemn or disenfranchise others. Regrettably, especially in recent years, such technological advances have been met by the growth of mistrust, suspicions, and even allegations of theft in some cases, leading to some breakdown in trust and cooperation. This trust gap has been met with the inability or unwillingness of politicians and leaders to initiate efforts to tackle the growing problem. Indeed, some would even promote mistrust on ideological grounds. So over time, we then start wondering if we can trust our machines better than we can trust each other, especially among nation states! This would be truly regrettable if we let our advances in technology be an impediment to our trust in humanities. If not handled properly, this trust gap may spiral out of control with unimaginable consequences.

The famous and revered Adam Smith, in his book *The Theory of Moral Sentiments* wrote: "Capitalism works best in societies when there are high levels of trust between its participants. When social trust falls, the cost of doing business rises. When trust goes, so many other things go too." In his other famous book *The Wealth of Nations*, he wrote: "It is in the progressive state, while society is advancing to the further acquisition, rather than when it has acquired the full complement of riches, that the condition of the labouring poor, of the great body of the people, seems to be the happiest and most comfortable." By this I think he meant that the vast majority of the working people, especially the poor, will be more than willing to participate and be a stakeholder in society, with a state of fulfilment and contentment, if they all have a common goal to aim at and to work for. In other words, the journey is just as important as the outcome, if not more so. This journey is a collective effort by all in a society which needs progress to reach richness. In my view, this progress in a society must involve trust too. This book was written in the 18th century but just as relevant now in the present world, arguably more so. We are all somewhat connected, and technology in the future will connect us even more. As a result, some political and social scientists have already started to comment on this phenomenon of trust gap. There are so many ways nowadays where trust is breached. Now one can simply take a look around at things like news, privacy, data, social media and one can then instantly question if trust is warranted. Yet, how do we address this trust gap? We cannot ask technology to solve this problem for us because trust is not programmable. We must do this ourselves and that means our leaders and statesmen will have to take and steer us all in this direction. So one of my statements in this chapter is that this trust shortage needs to be addressed urgently before it becomes too late.

The next question we should ask ourselves is: what sort of world we wish to live in, or more appropriately, what sort of world we would like our future generations to live in? What would we bequeath to them? In life, everything comes with a price and the price will not come down. Mobile phones will cost just as much except that they will be much better. With all the advances, there is a huge social cost to it. We now know getting clean air to breathe comes with a price whereas it was free to our ancestors in days gone by! The question is at what price are we willing to pay? The world will need fewer people to carry out the same tasks. Machines work on a 24/7 basis (such as booking a holiday in the middle of the night!), carrying out important tasks without any need for holidays or employment laws. The price will be factored in, to a very large degree, not on the practical side of the actual factory production cost of making the microchips but on the closely guarded secret of the intellectual property value involved in developing the microchips! It is not how much it costs to make that matter but how much to charge which the users are willing to accept, while factoring in the most favourable terms the value of the intellectual property associated with these.

The Price of Our Knowledge, Who Pays for it?

The principle of intellectual property is a fairly modern concept. It started in the 17th and 18th centuries but it has only started to assume its importance from the late 20th century. It gives due recognition, appreciation, and rewards, both in fame and fortune, for human ingenuity and endeavours in turning ideas into practical applications in our daily lives. In general, it can involve copyright, trademark, trade secrets, and patents. It also means there is a monetary interest or financial stake associated with it. Adam Smith, in producing his masterpiece *The Wealth of Nations*, probably did not take the idea of copyright too seriously in writing this remarkable book and yet his phenomenal contribution has been forever appreciated and studied by all of us. Trademark will be a marker for us to recognise, though not necessarily to buy its product. Logo will always be a logo! We will always know what Coca Cola or Sony is and how the brand is presented in its advertisements. Patent is where the profit issue comes in. Take for example a new anticancer drug which is targeted specifically to the cancer cells. The drug may mean years of research in the laboratories and then tested extensively before it can be licensed and produced en masse. The pharmaceutical which makes this drug will apply for a patent, which it hopes may be granted, say, for at least 10 years, so effectively it will have a monopoly on a worldwide sale of this drug. This patent is necessary, quite rightly, to recover the cost of research and development of the drug but it also provides the company with a unique opportunity to make a huge profit during this period of monopoly. No competitor will be allowed to eat into the profits. One real life example for this patent and the issue of profit was during the general election campaign in the UK in December 2019. There were very heated and controversial debates among the political parties, mainly on how the UK should start to engage in bilateral trade discussions with other countries and economic blocks, especially the USA. A document was leaked to the public that the US pharmaceutical properties were lobbying the US Government to put pricing and patency of their profitable drugs on the discussion agenda. So this question of patent will be on the agenda for negotiation, with the clear implication being the UK may then face a much higher cost for new drugs, irrespective of where they are made, as long as they are US owned. This point was hotly and anxiously discussed as currently these drugs are cheaper in the UK than the USA because of the collective purchasing power of the UK representing NHS on the whole. Once you have the answer to how much to charge for the drug on the market, protected by patent, the financial rewards can be huge as this can even surpass national boundaries. The techno giants, just like the pharmaceutical giants, are in a similar position because they help us to connect in real time with the world, even talking or videoing everyone we like to, be it families or friends. In my view therefore, the words intellectual property do have another meaning here. It confers a tone of being overtly possessive of property and in this context, property means not just wealth but excessive wealth. Furthermore, this wealth will be concentrated on the shareholders and the senior executives who would have share options. Fortunes are therefore made. There is a difference, morally speaking, between a reasonable profit in recognition for the intellectual effort associated with it and a reasonable investment return as profits. The difference is to achieve appreciation and motivation on the one hand and profiteering on the other hand. Some investment funds label this balance between the two as ethical investments, though being commercially naive, I have no insight on what this balance means in practice. Most of us, living in a maturing economy, are living as middle classes and as such, we are willing to exercise our choice, if the need so requires, to pay a premium for anything that would make our life more comfortable and connected. Or, if we are ill and faced with a life-threatening condition, we will naturally wish for the latest drug to be available for us as well. After all, this is all we have always hoped to achieve while working hard for a living, to have some comfort in life and the health to enjoy the comfort. The middle-class aspirations may ironically be the middle-class trap!

The Social Cost of Changes

Following the train of thought above, it is not difficult to surmise that all these very desirable and great advances will have another flaw, which is now also being openly discussed among economists, and social and political scientists. While these advances are available to those who can afford it in monetary terms, they all come with a hefty social price. This is no free lunch. Nowadays nearly all predict that employment for the poor and unskilled will be massively reduced. Human labour will be displaced and replaced by the combinations of AI, big data, and robots. In addition, it is also likely that not only labour demand will be less, the inequality in income will be much greater than any time in human history. The emergence of progressive income inequality, a trend that has been accelerating in recent years, is almost universally recognised by all political scientists. Like a pop star, you only need one worldwide hit and you and the recording company are set for life. They call this income inequality the 1% and the 99%. It means 1% of the population owns most of the wealth while the rest is shared among the remaining 99%. It is so ironic and extremely discomforting to note that right after the financial crisis in 2008, the ordering of state-of-the-art, top notched, luxuriously-designed, super yachts was not reduced but actually increased, highlighting the emergence of a new class called the super-rich with wealth that few can possibly imagine So how should we, as masters of the universe, look at the problems and deal with them?

This brings me to my other statement. What do we mean by skilled labour? It is often said that in the future, just like what was discussed previously, the world would need more skills such as software engineers, financial analysts, AI developers, and big data analysts while there is less a need for manual labour such as traffic wardens, patrolling police officers, train drivers, air traffic controllers, bin collectors, or road sweepers. While I tend to agree with this, I beg to offer a different interpretation on the meaning of skilled labour. AI works best when there is a clearly defined goal from a collection of data. It is entirely foreseeable that in the near future, the world will still need manual labour. The buzzword these days that everyone is talking about is knowledge-based economy, which seems to imply a certain degree of high skill. The point is, this knowledge-based economy, while without doubt has its huge benefits, does not actually replace manual skill, which itself is a kind of knowledge on its own. Humanities need all skills, and not let one skillset disenfranchise another skillset. Creative destruction does happen, such as VHS tapes, Kodak films, or even music CDs but this destruction is unlikely to displace human skills because of our ability to adapt. Our house, either owned or rented, will be our sanctuary, our comfort zone. These sanctuaries or zones need upkeep, so we will need skills such as painters and decorators for our house, a plumber to unblock a drain, and some even need house maids to clean our house, cleaners for our windows, and gardeners for our gardens. In short, estate management skills are still needed, and I can't see how smart machines can be so advanced that they can even cross the boundary to come managing our house, which nearly all of us would view as our most valuable material possession. These people, often labelled as unskilled labour (which for me, is a misnomer, as I think they are anything but unskilled), non-middle class, learn their trades by apprenticeship and not by professional or tertiary qualifications. In some countries, such as Germany and Scandinavia, government initiatives are already in place to provide genuine vocational skills. These people, once trained, can become in the near future the skilled ones that the world needs. Equally, societies and communities need others to help too. So, we may need fewer taxi drivers, but we will still need police officers, doctors, nurses, teachers, firefighters, and care assistants for our nursing homes.

Therefore, in my view, the distinction between the professional or white-collar workers, known commonly as the middle class, and the manual labour, known by some as the working class, will be much less clear in this new world. Machines can provide efficiency, accuracy, productivity, and obedience while we humans can provide human touch as we have cognitive functions, our feelings and our compassion for our fellow human beings. Robots so far have not been able to do so, not even close. AI can beat the best grandmaster in a game of chess anytime, anywhere, but it will never savour the joy of success or misery of failure. Robots or big data or AI only have updates but do not have friends, nor peers, nor communities, but we humans do. We strive for harmony and a state of equilibrium and equality, and in so doing feel better about ourselves. To get the best of both worlds, we must value what the human touch can offer and how different it is from the machines. This human touch, collectively in a society called civic values, is often taken for granted presently. Perhaps it will change when machines are around the corner to run our lives and threaten our very own existence.

I have never subscribed to the idea of class, be it upper, middle, or working class. These are very narrowly and ideologically defined for political reasons. It may have served its purpose during the times of aristocracy, of clergymen, of nobility and peasantry, but it has passed its sell-by date. My personal take on this is that it really matters not what class one is in. We should be living in a classless society. What really matters is how good one is at doing one's job. A doctor seeing a patient in the clinic, a lawyer advising his clients, is just as important to me as the plumber who unblocks my drain. Skills of any sort should transcend boundaries, based on needs and not on class.

A Shift in the Centre of Gravity

Unlike the past few hundreds of years, when the West dominated political thinking and its system of governance, backed up by their technological superiority and fuelled by their colonial aggression, I believe also that it is entirely possible that many of the questions facing humanity can be answered partially by what is happening in China, India, and Africa, as these three large countries and continents, and their population, start to catch up with modernity.

For China and its medical services, I have no doubt that it will improve through changes and reforms, because not only are these the will of the government and the people, it is also because the technology is already there in China and in some cases, being tried out and implemented. Home-grown cutting-edge drug manufacturing is being developed, digital medical services are now available to cut down the physical distance between users and providers, clinical data will be more complete, and state medical insurance will be much more equal between the regions as China becomes more prosperous. I am hopeful about these; it is not only possible but probable too. I remain positive and am convinced the new frontier is on the horizon, more so now than when I first arrived in China eight years ago. Furthermore, I have already mentioned briefly in Chapters 10 and 22 the difference in various healthcare systems, all with their unique strengths. The NHS in the UK is admired globally for its strong and fair primary care system, equal access, and its health promotion effort. The USA is world beating in terms of its basic science approach, its long-established innovation, and its translational research. China, because of its huge population and its huge investments in application technology in the last few decades, will offer substantial data-based knowledge in our understanding and the study of diseases, in public health such as infection prevention and control, early screening of cancer and diabetes, and the use of telemedicine and smart technology in connecting up the users and providers, and cutting down the geographical distance between the two, thus day to day the provision of medical services can be real time, weatherproof and traffic proof, with built-in best practice guide. These modern endeavours will require real human desires for collaboration and not competition, achievement of common good and not institutional fame, sharing of knowledge rather than monopolising knowledge. Each system has a great deal to offer, and the sum is bigger than its parts. So, can we do it? And I would say, yes, we can!

So, what now?

By recognising the needs of society, of nation states, and their national interests, I hope and I do believe human ingenuity will work out the right balance, much like the current global efforts we are now witnessing in protecting the environment and dealing with climate change. The key thing for us is to be vigilant of the upsides as well as downsides. Even though in the history of the world there were famines, starvation, and wars, it is undeniable that humanities have over the last thousands of years evolved to the extent we all feel the world is better than before, we have a better life than our ancestors. Our life expectancy is longer, our health is better, and our food supply, by and large, is adequate to feed the ever-increasing global population. We must also continue to leverage ourselves on our ingenuity and ability to offer not only invention, but also compassion, working side by side with AI and other technologies, being fully appreciative of our own uniqueness while enjoying the advantages that AI and technology can offer. We should not be fearful of but be prepared for creative destruction by constantly trying to create more.

We, the homo sapiens, began our journey, estimated at 400,000 years ago, somewhere near the present-day Ethiopia. We have since evolved over many, many years to reach where we are now. And, given how the lives of our ancestors had been changed compared to the present days, we should expect further evolutionary changes, and must look into the future with some degree of confidence, not forgetting the ultimate aim and the wish of all our human endeavours, discovered, invented, and sustained, are for the benefit of mankind, just like our ancestors. That should be our only benchmark.

EPILOGUE

MEN IN THE ARENA

(to share with all the people I work with at HKU SZH)

It is not the critic who counts; not the man who points out how the strong man stumbles, or where the doer of deeds could have done them better. The credit belongs to the man who is actually in the arena, whose face is marred by dust and sweat and blood; who strives valiantly; who errs, who comes short again and again, because there is no effort without error and shortcoming; but who does actually strive to do the deeds; who knows great enthusiasms, the great devotions; who spends himself in a worthy cause; who at the best knows in the end the triumph of high achievement, and who at the worst, if he fails, at least fails while daring greatly, so that his place shall never be with those cold and timid souls who neither know victory nor defeat.

Theodore Roosevelt, Sorbonne, Paris, 1910.

RECOMMENDED READING LIST

1. *The Search for Modern China*
By Jonathan Spence, published by W.W. Norton & Company 2001

2. *The Clash of Civilization: And the Remaking of World Order*
By Samuel Huntington, published by Simon and Schuster UK 2002

3. *Have a Little Faith*
By Mitch Albom, published by Sphere 2010

4. *Factory Girls: Voices from the Heart of Modern China*
By Leslie Chang, published by Picador 2010

5. *When China Rules the World: The End of the Western World and the Birth of a New Global Power*
By Martin Jacques, published by Penguin 2012

6. *On China*
By Henry Kissinger, published by Penguin 2012

7. *The End of History and the Last Man*
By Francis Fukuyama, published by Penguin 2012

8. *What Money Can't Buy: The Moral Limits of Markets*
By Michael Sandel, published by Penguin 2013

9. *China Goes Global: The Partial Power*
By David Shambaugh, published by Oxford University Press 2014

10. *The Analects* (Penguin Classics)
By Confucius, published by Penguin Classics 2014

11. *The Wisdom of Confucius*
By Epiphanius Wislon, published by CreateSpace Independent Platform 2015

12. *Sapiens: A Brief History of Humankind*
By Yuval Noah Hahari, published by Vintage 2015

13. *Dealing with China*
By Hank Paulson, published by Headline 2016

14. *The Silk Road: A New History of the World*
By Peter Frankopan, published by Bloomsbury Paperback, 2016

15. *Wealth and Power: China's Long March to the Twenty-first Century*
By Orville Schell, published by Abacus 2016

16. *The Retreat of Western Liberalism*
By Edward Luce, published by Abacus 2018

17. *China: Fragile Power*

By Susan Shirk, published by Oxford University Press 2018

18. *The Virtue of Nationalism*

By Yoram Hazony, published by Basic Books 2018

19. *Bad Blood: Secrets and Lies in a Silicon Valley Startup*

By John Carreyrou, published by Picador 2019

20. *AI Superpowers: China, Silicon Valley and the New World Order*

By Kai-Fu Li, published by Houghton Mifflin Harcourt 2019

21. *The Penguin History of Modern China: The Fall and Rise of a Great Power* (1950 to Present)

By Jonathan Fenby, published by Penguin, 3rd edition 2019

22. *Sovereignty in China: A Genealogy of a Concept since 1840* (Cambridge Studies in International and Comparative Law Book 141)

By Maria Carrai, published by Cambridge University Press 2019.

Printed in Great Britain
by Amazon